Two Brown

ENVELOPES

Two Brown
ENVELOPES

How to Shrug Off Setbacks,
Bounce Back from Failure and
Build a Global Business

HAZEM MULHIM

TWO BROWN ENVELOPES

*How to Shrug Off Setbacks, Bounce Back from Failure
and Build a Global Business*

ISBN   978-1-5445-2483-2   *Hardcover*

           978-1-5445-2481-8   *Paperback*

           978-1-5445-2482-5   *Ebook*

CONTENTS

Introduction .... *ix*

1. Watching My Father *1*

2. Two Brown Envelopes *15*

3. Behind the Iron Curtain *27*

4. My First Business *39*

5. The First Gulf War, Bankruptcy & Survival *51*

6. The Richest Man in the World *65*

7. INSEAD, Blue Oceans & Accelerated Growth *79*

8. Turning European *99*

9. When the IFC Picked Up the Phone *111*

10. The Day Interpol Came Knocking on My Door 123

11. The Realignment Years...135

12. Edward Snowden, the NSA & Me 147

13. Looking To The Future..159

14. Why I Do What I Do 171

15. The Eight Secrets for Bouncing Back from Failure..............183

    Acknowledgments..195

    Endnotes...199

To my parents, Laila and Mohammed,
who made me the man I am.

INTRODUCTION

THE DAY MY FATHER INVITED ME TO HIS OFFICE IN KUWAIT AND showed me two brown envelopes is a day I will never forget. I was twenty years old at the time, and although I didn't know it then, it was the crucial turning point in my life—the fork in the river when I could have traveled in any number of directions. As I sat before him, waiting to be spoken to, I wondered what was inside those envelopes on his desk. One seemed fuller than the other. I soon found out—and what I did next, after I left my father's office, determined the rest of my life.

All these years later, I still get a momentary flashback when I'm suddenly back in that office with my father and those two brown envelopes. This happened most vividly when I was strolling through the streets of Tokyo with a friend a few years ago. It was May, and although the cherry blossom season had passed, there was nevertheless a great national celebration. Everywhere I looked, I noticed there were hundreds of little flags fluttering in the wind. They each bore the distinctive features of a fish. I wondered why. I assumed the fish was salmon and celebrated the Japanese fondness for sushi.

Rather intrigued, I asked my friend, "Why are there flags with salmon flying from every pole?" He laughed and put me right. The fish was not salmon but carp, and the flags, or rather wind socks, were *koinobori*—"carp streamers"—and they celebrated Golden Week, the longest Japanese holiday. The carp was chosen because it is respected for its strength, its spirit and its perseverance, swimming against the fast-flowing stream, just like salmon.

Somehow, in my mind, the brightly colored *koinobori* intertwined with the two brown envelopes. From the day I stepped outside my father's office, I have found myself swimming against the tide. It is, I think, the defining feature of the entrepreneur.

And it is to describe what it takes to be an entrepreneur that I have written this book.

* * *

I am not a famous billionaire entrepreneur like Bill Gates or Elon Musk. In fact, you have probably never heard of me—unless, of course, you happen to run one of the eight hundred financial institutions that use the compliance, risk-management, cybersecurity and anti-money laundering services of the company I founded nearly forty years ago.

So why, you may ask, should you listen to me? Why should you bother reading this book?

My story is—ultimately—a story of success. Those eight hundred financial institutions—headquartered in the United States, Middle East, Europe and Asia—constitute almost 10 percent of the world's banks. I started out as a shop owner, opening the first computer store in Jordan in the early 1980s, when I was still in my twenties. From those relatively humble beginnings, I evolved my business, moving out of computer sales and into software services, with operations not only in Jordan but also Dubai, Egypt and Turkey. Today, my business is spread across Europe, the Middle East and the United States, and my clients are spread around the world.

But if, when summarized in a paragraph, my business has been on an ever-growing trajectory, the reality is somewhat different. My story is also a story of the downs as well as the ups.

Failure is a touchy subject for many business leaders. It is seen as a sign of frailty, a mark of weakness. But in my view, failure is an occupational hazard of an entrepreneur's life. If you haven't failed, you haven't lived—and you certainly can't hope to succeed.

The big challenge is to learn from the setbacks. You will read many books on entrepreneurship that preach the importance of resilience, perseverance, adaptability and the steely resolve to triumph against the odds. You will not find me disagreeing with them. But I have never found them particularly useful.

The books I have found most illuminating and truly inspiring are those that give you a real sense of what it's like to *feel* the highs of winning after enduring the humbling lows of defeat. The authors take you with them on their journey. You stand, as it were, on their shoulders, watching as they take their decisions, suffer setbacks and enjoy their victories. That's the kind of book

I've tried to write here. I've made millions of dollars—and lost millions of dollars too. I've been virtually bankrupt—and I've found a way to bounce back. It has been tough at times. It has been painful for me and for my family. No entrepreneur comes through unscathed.

But I wouldn't have it any other way. In fact, there really isn't another way. Either you *are* an entrepreneur or you're not. You can't *become* one. Yes, you can pick up some entrepreneurial skills. But entrepreneurs are made long before they choose the life of an entrepreneur. From an early age, they see the world differently, they ask tricky questions, they push against convention, they draw connections between apparently unconnected things, they take absurd risks, they make mistakes, and they learn from them.

I was twenty-nine years old when I founded what is now called Eastnets. Back then, I was full of optimism. Today, all these years later, I remain full of optimism. Everywhere, I see opportunities, not challenges. I see "blue oceans" of uncontested undiscovered markets. I see that the future is bright for those who are temperamentally suited, like those Japanese *koinobori*, to swim against the tide.

If you are an entrepreneur, then you should recognize some of your own story in this book. If you are planning to start a business, then you should get a real sense of the roller coaster that will be your life. But if there is a universality about my story, there is also a uniqueness. Indeed, every entrepreneur's story is unique, particular to them.

My story started being written long before I was born.

Chapter 1

WATCHING MY FATHER

IF YOU CLIMB TO THE HIGHEST INHABITED POINT IN PALESTINE, you come to a small town called Halhul. Rising nearly one thousand meters above the Mediterranean Sea, it stands on the west bank of the Jordan River, surrounded by the peaks of the Hebron Mountains. It is a truly magical place. In winter, it is frozen by snow, as temperatures plummet to subzero. Indeed, there is one story that the word "Halhul" comes from an old Canaanite word meaning "to tremble (from the cold)." But in summer, the sun beats down, stirring the landscape into life and creating a wonderfully fertile place that produces an abundance of grapes, olives, milk and, yes, honey.

I first set eyes on Halhul—the land of my fathers—when I was five years old. The year was 1960. Although my family had lived there since time immemorial, my own father, Mohammed, had been forced into exile after the *Nakba*—the "catastrophe" which saw 700,000 Palestinians flee or be forcibly moved from their homeland after the creation of Israel in 1948. In the Arab-Israeli war that decided how Palestine would be carved up, Halhul—

now part of the Israeli-occupied Palestinian territory of the West Bank—was annexed by Jordan.

As a result, my father—born in Palestine when it was administered by the British—became a Jordanian citizen. So did I, although I was born in Saudi Arabia, where my parents had moved after my father secured a job with Aramco, the Arabia American Oil Company.

When I first visited Halhul, we traveled from Amman, Jordan's capital, where we lived after hurriedly returning from Saudi Arabia. I was just a toddler when we left Dhahran, my birthplace and the town (now city) overlooking the Persian Gulf where Aramco was, and still is, headquartered. So, of course, I have no memory of the move. But I feel sure that it left an indelible mark on me and the way I look at things. I left the place where I was born and moved on to a large bustling capital that was a world away from my ancestral home. And, ever since then, I have not stopped moving on.

That is the life of an exile.

As Edward Said, the renowned Palestinian academic who made his home in America, once wrote: "Exile is never the state of being satisfied, placid, or secure.... It is nomadic, decentered, contrapuntal."[1]

* * *

In this regard, I was following in the footsteps of my father. He was born in Halhul in 1927, the scion of a long line of illiterate peasants who had farmed on the slopes of Mount Nabi Yunis for generations. For four hundred years, the land had been ruled by the Ottoman Turks. But following the collapse of the Ottoman Empire after the First World War, Britain assumed administrative control of Palestine, starting in 1920. This was Mohammed Mulhim's good fortune. A bright child, he was a star pupil at school, and in 1946, he was one of eight Palestinians to win a scholarship to a British university.[2]

One of his contemporaries, Edmond Asfour, who would later become a Lebanese diplomat, studied moral sciences at Oxford. But five of the scholars studied law, including my father, who went to university in Leeds. There, in one of England's great industrial cities in the north of the country, he completed not only an undergraduate degree but also a master's degree, graduating with an LLM in 1950. Subsequently, he was called to the bar by Gray's Inn, one of the distinguished associations of barristers in the heart of London. Suddenly, he was thrust into the upper echelon of British society. At Gray's Inn, he was able to rub shoulders, metaphorically speaking, with the likes of Sir Winston Churchill and Franklin D. Roosevelt, who had themselves only recently been elected honorary benchers of this, the most aristocratic of the four Inns of Court.

This success must have given him the steely confidence he showed throughout his life. But after four years in England, he returned home to an uncertain future. That was because the world had changed—or, at least, *his* world had changed. Palestine, the country he had left as an eighteen-year-old, no longer existed. King Abdullah I, the Jordanian king, now ruled his homeland—not the British. Returning to Halhul, my father briefly tried to make a living, setting up a marketing cooperative to support farmers and protect them from the feudal tendencies of landlords. But after one year, when a job offer from Aramco came, he jumped at the opportunity.

Aramco was responsible for tapping Saudi Arabia's vast reserves of oil, which had been discovered in the early 1930s not far from Dhahran, after the biggest oil strike in history. The company—jointly owned by four American oil companies that would become known as Chevron, Texaco, Exxon and Mobil— held the concession to dig beneath Saudi Arabia's truly golden sands. Of course, while the Americans were in day-to-day charge, the Saudi king always held the casting vote in any decision. Accordingly, in the wake of Israel's creation, Ibn Saud, the founder and first king of Saudi Arabia, instructed Aramco to hire one thousand Palestinian refugees. My father, with his legal expertise and his facility in Arabic and English, was one of these new recruits.[3]

It was a dream job. But he soon found that he did not see eye to eye with Aramco's American bosses. Four years in postwar Britain—years that saw Clement Atlee's Labour Party sweep into power (defeating Churchill's Conservative Party) and attempt to rebuild a country exhausted by war through bold welfare reform, such as the National Health Service—had left a deep impression on him. As a result, when he returned to the Middle East, he was astonished by what he found. As he later put it: in the UK, he was offered "access to diverse opinions and a democratic milieu within which our freedom to differ in opinions is tolerated." So it was "a shock…to come back to the Middle East in 1951."[4]

In Saudi Arabia, Aramco had created a kind of segregated city.[5] This, remember, was a time when segregation was a feature of daily life in many American cities, with "Whites Only" notices often barring the way to African Americans. In Dhahran, there was an "American camp"—a kind of gated community that housed the company's American bosses and other senior staff, including my father and mother, and me when I arrived in 1955— and an "Arab camp." The two compounds, which were separated by barbed wire, were quite different. The American compound was, as visitors reported, like a slice of small-town America, with a swimming pool (the first in Saudi Arabia), a theater, a bowling alley, tennis courts and even a baseball diamond. By contrast, the Arab compound, which sat in the shadow of the Dhahran *jabals*, was pockmarked by concrete tin-roofed shacks and lacked even the basic amenities of life such as fresh running water, power and functional sewers. In the summer heat, the lack of air-conditioning units meant that workers routinely moved their beds outside at night to sleep under the stars.

With his pronounced sense of fairness, my father supported the Saudi and other Arab workers as they protested their slum-like living conditions. In 1953, this led to strikes, with thirteen thousand people putting down their tools and refusing to work.[6] And three years later, there were riots. For Aramco's bosses, this was the last straw. In a striking admission, the company's own official history notes: "Many company officials categorized the petitioners as discontented dreamers and intellectuals who, after a taste of what the West had to offer, were now dissatisfied."[7] The company singled out the ringleaders, including my father, and after six years in Saudi Arabia, he left Aramco on bad terms, moving the family to Amman.

In his first year back in Jordan, he worked as the legal counsel for the Ministry of Economics. But this was not where he saw his future. In Saudi Arabia, he had found his vocation. He was passionate about defending the downtrodden, and so he gave up his steady job in the government and started his own legal practice, speaking up for labor rights and often taking on *pro bono* cases. I learned a lesson from this: listen to your instincts, follow your passions, stay true to yourself.

As my father built up his business, he gave his children—me, my two brothers and one sister—the kind of education that is the perfect preparation for the life of an entrepreneur. And by "education," I don't simply mean "schooling," although that was very good too. Rather, I mean "experiences."

* * *

Looking back, Amman, and the whole region, was the ideal location for the budding entrepreneur. Here, for centuries—in fact, for millennia—people have conducted trade as part of a global network. Palestine, the land located in the Levant between the Mediterranean and the Jordan River, is situated at the end of what was the 5,000-mile Silk Road from China. Some merchants would take the land route, passing through Syria to the Palestine coast; others would take the sea route and eventually sail up the Persian Gulf or Red Sea and then complete the final leg of the journey on camels, traveling overland through Palestine and on to Europe.

In Roman times, the route through Palestine was studded by a series of ten major cities—the Decapolis. Strung out like pearls, they served as trading posts, stopovers linking the East and the West. The furthest south was Philadelphia, modern-day Amman. The furthest north was Damascus, the capital of modern Syria. Vibrant, diverse, multicultural, wealthy, their presence continues to resonate to this day.

When you step into one of their bazaars, you are reminded of the rich business heritage of the region. I was taken to these wondrous, cacophonous markets from an early age. My grandmother—my mother's mother—often invited me to accompany her on her shopping trips. As I reflect now, those trips were my first lesson in raw entrepreneurialism.

She came from a long line of merchants. Her father ran a successful fruit and vegetable business in Jerusalem. After 1948, he reestablished his business in Beirut, later moving to Kuwait and Sharjah, and he developed a far-reaching export business in the Philippines and Kenya. Meanwhile, one of my grandmother's brothers emigrated to Chile, built his own fruit-and-vegetable business, and today one of his sons (my grandmother's nephew), Mohammed Abu-Ghazaleh, owns Fresh Del Monte Produce, one of the world's biggest grocery businesses.

Coming from this background, my grandmother knew how to haggle, how to bargain, and how to close a deal. Almost always, she would start by demanding an audacious fifty percent cut in the price. Typically, the market stall owner would scoff, with a dismissive wave of the hand and a pained expression that seemed to say, "Are you out of your mind?" But when she turned on her heel and started to walk, he would implore her to come back with a new, lower price. Eventually, after this commercial quickstep, which may last for two or three minutes, they usually came to a mutually agreed price. It was exhausting to watch, and sometimes I had to hide, so embarrassed was I by my grandmother's brazen actions. But she always came away from those exchanges with a smile—and a sense of victory. And I am sure I learned something of what I know now from those visits to the bazaars of Jerusalem, and later Beirut and Amman. Of course, at the age of five or six, I was not taking notes. But I certainly understood that there is no such thing as a fixed price. Yes, a product or service might have an intrinsic value, but this is not the only thing that determines price. Also important are the context of the sale—whether it is a market, a shop, or some other place—and the circumstances of the buyer and the seller: does the buyer want the product, no matter what the price is, or does the seller need to off-load the product because they are strapped for cash? These things can be discerned by, among other things, a careful observation of behavior, tone of voice and body language. Ultimately, you learn that everything's negotiable. You have to bargain. You have to ask, "What's the *second* price?"

* * *

During the summer, when I wasn't trailing my grandmother through the markets, I was often sent away to see my relatives in Halhul. For most of my childhood, as the son of a successful lawyer, I lived the life of a pampered city boy. This is why my father was keen for me to be connected to my roots—to the family who remained farmers and never left the West Bank. We drove up through the mountains, often stopping for lunch at a restaurant opposite Damascus Gate in Jerusalem, and then we continued to Bethlehem and, eventually, Halhul. When I was there, it was like stepping back in time: people lived closer to the land, and while life was hard and very physical, the pace of everything was slower. The vehicle of choice was not the tractor but the mule.

On one of my visits—I think it was 1961, when I was six years old—I went to Halhul with my mother, Laila. That time, my father did not come. That's because he was in jail. An outspoken lawyer, and a member of the lawyers' union, he had been rounded up along with many other political activists after the young Jordanian king, Hussein, still only in his midtwenties, imposed martial law.

While we were in Halhul, we discovered that King Hussein would be visiting, as part of his tour of the kingdom. I don't know how this happened, but it was arranged that I would meet the king and beg him to release my father. On the appointed day— one that I will never forget—I was given a wooden box containing a dove. Moments later, I was standing before the king, and in a carefully choreographed exchange, I opened the box, released the dove, and said, "Please release my father, as I now release this dove!"

With a proverbial click of his fingers, the king consented to my request, and when I returned to Amman, I was happily reunited with my father.

But it would not be the last time that my father was thrown into jail. In 1966, he was again rounded up with other lawyers. This time, he was taken to a harsher military prison. This might have weakened the resolve of a lesser man. But the thing I remember about my father is that he always came out of jail with a big smile. If he was hurting inside, he never let it show. He never looked cowed. He never looked despondent.

His approach taught me about persistence, about perseverance. Whatever life throws at you, you should stay positive, you should look forward, you should keep your eyes trained on the horizon.

* * *

On June 5, 1967, my father was still incarcerated when Israel went to war with Egypt, Syria and Jordan. Six days later, the war was over, and Israel, not yet twenty years old as a nation, marched into its neighbors' lands and seized control of the Gaza Strip along the Mediterranean coast, the Sinai Peninsula, the Golan Heights, and Jordan's territories in the West Bank, including East Jerusalem and Halhul.

In the wake of this conflict, my father was released from prison, and he resolved to move the family from Jordan. He knew that, with Israel ruling his homeland, life would change. For me, there would be no more summer visits to Halhul, no more trips to the bazaars of Jerusalem with my grandmother.

It was time to move on.

The place he chose was Kuwait, the tiny city-state on the banks of the Persian Gulf. He could not have picked a better place.

For much of the twentieth century, Kuwait had been a British protectorate since it was regarded as strategically important, providing safe passage for ships going to and from India, then the jewel in Britain's imperial crown. As a result, it became recognized as one of the most liberal countries in the region. When the British left in 1961, the amir built on these liberal foundations, and Kuwait entered a period that historians have depicted as "a golden age." In 1963, Kuwait became the first Arab state in the Persian Gulf to establish a constitution and parliament, and by the time we arrived, there was a palpable sense of having reached an open, modern, multicultural metropolis.

When we got to Kuwait, however, we were not alone. After the Six-Day War, some 300,000 Palestinians were forced to abandon their homes, and many went to Kuwait. Back in 1948, when Palestine was wiped off the map, many Palestinians had fled to Kuwait, and we thought of this country as a kind of second home. One of my uncles—one of my mother's brothers—was a senior executive at Kuwait Airways, and he helped my father secure a job as the legal adviser to the Kuwait Insurance Company.

Eventually, my father tired of this corporate role, and as in Jordan, he set up his own legal practice. Meanwhile, I went back to school. In Jordan, I had attended the Collège De La Salle—Frères, a private school run by Christian priests. It was strict. Lessons were taught in Arabic, English and French. And by the time I moved to Kuwait, I was well prepared for the next phase of schooling.

In Kuwait, I was sent to two schools—Al-Jamil, which was private, and Abdullah Al-Salem, which was public, something of an academic hothouse, and where I moved when I was fifteen years old. My parents were delighted that I had managed to secure entry to this competitive academy, but I remember that I had to work exceedingly hard to keep up. This, of course, pleased my father, who was a stickler for discipline and diligence. In the West, people talk about the Protestant work ethic. But in the Middle East, there is a similar emphasis on the need to work hard in order to get on. Growing up, I could not fail to notice the words from the Qur'an—the 105th verse of chapter 9 entitled *sūrat l-tawbah*, or "The Repentance"—that my father had put on one of the walls at home: "You have to work, and your work will be seen by God, by the Prophet, and by all the Believers."

Throughout my school days, we were encouraged to read widely—a habit I have continued to this day. Bill Gates, Microsoft's co-founder, is famously effusive about the importance of reading for stretching one's mind. He consumes about fifty books every year—everything from literary fiction to science and history. "Every book teaches me something new or helps me see things differently," he once said. "Reading fuels a sense of curiosity about the world."[8] I fully concur. In my teenage years in Kuwait, I traveled far and wide through books. No doubt inspired by my father's social conscience and fascination with the plight of the poor and oppressed, I read Victor Hugo's *Les Misérables* and Charles Dickens' *Oliver Twist*. The Russian Maxim Gorky was another writer whose work I read avidly as a boy. H.G. Wells' *A Short History of the World* was on my bookshelf, and I enjoyed its whistle-stop tour through the great events of the past. Among Arab writers, Taha Hussein, the brilliant, blind, French-educated, Egyptian writer was, and remains, a particular favorite of mine.

But if books transported me far from Kuwait, what I remember most from my years there—from 1967 to 1973—are the foreign holidays, or rather *adventures*, with my family. My reading broadened my horizons *intellectually*, but my traveling broadened them *literally*. Every time I think back to those formative years, I am reminded of the observation of Oliver Wendell Holmes, the American polymath and father of the famous Supreme Court Justice: "Every now and then, a man's mind is stretched by a new idea…and never shrinks back to its former dimension."[9] It is so true.

We would pack the car as if we were going on a long expedition, and then we would follow the roads to all the great capitals of the region. My father would tell us about the history of the different places as we ticked them off: Damascus, the northernmost city of the Decapolis and the strategically important center for the Islamic caliphates, in particular the Umayyad, who made it their capital; Beirut, the home of the ancient Phoenicians and now the capital of Lebanon, which we were told was "the Switzerland of the Arab world"; Cairo, with its astonishing pyramids; Baghdad, with its links back to the first civilizations in ancient Mesopotamia and the remarkable ruins of the Greeks and Romans; and Istanbul, with its memory of Byzantium, Roman Constantinople and the Ottoman Empire.

Today, these journeys seem so exotic, so romantic. The idea that you could drive to all these places seems outlandish now—it just would not be feasible in the current geopolitical climate. I certainly feel fortunate that I was able to experience these different Middle Eastern cultures. Those journeys opened my eyes not only to lost ancient worlds but also to new and different modern worlds, and to a world of possibilities. Nothing, it seemed, was out of reach.

Except for one place: Halhul.

Throughout my time in Kuwait, we did return to Jordan, but we were never able to get to my father's birthplace, we were never able to spend time with our extended family. Under Israeli rule, Halhul was pretty much off-limits.

But then, in 1972, we did, finally, get a visa to go home for a short visit. I was seventeen years old. I hadn't set eyes on the beautiful hills surrounding Halhul for five years, and little did I know then that I wouldn't see them again for a long, long time.

I would only return after I had turned thirty, set up a business and become a father myself.

Chapter 2

TWO BROWN ENVELOPES

I GREW UP WITH MY FATHER TELLING ME ALL ABOUT HIS formative years in England in the late 1940s. It was a time of scarcity: there were no luxuries, rationing still existed, and austerity was the prevailing economic orthodoxy. And yet my father was filled with hope as he watched a nation try to rebuild itself anew in the aftermath of the Second World War. He was energized by the Labour leader, Clement Atlee, excited by the creation of the National Health Service, and enthused by ideas about workers' rights and the cooperative movement. He was animated by the new mood of freedom that followed the defeat of Nazism, and he applauded the efforts of anti-colonial leaders—notably Mahatma Gandhi and Nehru in India—who fought for independence from the British Empire.

He enjoyed his four years as a law student in Leeds, and he knew that the experience had set him up for success in life. Everywhere he went, he carried his business card, stamped with the words: "Barrister-at-Law, Gray's Inn." He was justly proud of his achievement. Step inside Gray's Inn's ancient hall, with its ornate oak screen, which is said to have been carved from wood salvaged from a defeated galleon of the Spanish Armada and given to the lawyers by Queen Elizabeth I, and you can see how far my father traveled in those postwar years.[10] And so it was inevitable that, when it came to my own postschool education, England would loom large as an option.

It is important to note here that Palestinians regard education as a critical asset. As a people, we are defined not by our faith— since there are Palestinian Muslims, Palestinian Christians and Palestinian Jews—but by the place we called home until we were brutally forced to leave in 1948. Since then, there has been nowhere that we can truly call home—where we rule ourselves. That loss continues to haunt us. How could it not? If you're an American, can you imagine being banished from entering the United States? If you're British, can you imagine having to apply for a visa in order to see the White Cliffs of Dover?

Without a home, we are, by definition, homeless. But with an education, at least, we can go anywhere, we can do anything, and we can succeed. As Yasser Arafat, the late Chairman of the Palestinian Liberation Organization (PLO), once put it, after 1948, "we had to struggle for sheer existence," and so "even in exile we educated our children." Why? "This was all a part of trying to survive."[11]

So Palestinian parents prioritize education, and they are prepared to set aside considerable resources to fund their children's schooling. That they do so is well known across the region. When Saudi Arabia's founder, King Ibn Sa'ud, ordered Aramco to hire Palestinians, he did so primarily because he wanted to show "a sign of solidarity" with displaced fellow Arabs. But he also knew that he would be able to tap what Aramco's official history recognized as "among the best-educated Arab populations in the Middle East."[12]

As I prepared to leave my Kuwaiti high school, I had several possible options. One was to go to university in the United States, which was the route taken by some of my friends. Another option was to go to either the American University in Beirut or the American University in Cairo—two institutions founded by American missionaries and which enjoyed fine reputations. But after much debate, it was decided that I would be sent to an English boarding school to study A-levels and prepare for entry to a British university.

* * *

So in 1973, when I was eighteen years old, I flew from Kuwait to London, landing in Heathrow on a cold September day. It was my first visit to Europe. Until then, the most distant place I had visited was Istanbul. After a couple of days in London, where I stayed with my mother's uncle, who was then working for an American investment company on Regent's Street, I took the train to a little town in Leicestershire called Market Harborough. Take a look at a map, as I did before I set off from Kuwait, and you'll see that it is slap bang in the middle of the country.

If you have never been to Market Harborough, think of a classic English town, with half-timbered Tudor buildings, and you'll know what I mean. Every time I think back to my first visit, I am reminded of the Hollywood movie *Straw Dogs*, in which the Dustin Hoffman character moves to an out-of-the-way English village in the middle of nowhere.

When I got to Market Harborough, after two hours on the train from London, it was 5 p.m. and already getting dark. The place was dead. Not long before, I had been weaving my way through the crowd as I looked for my carriage at Kings Cross station. Now, there was no one around except the stationmaster, who greeted me with a grunt, clipped my ticket and pointed me in the direction of the taxi stand. There, I waited for what seemed like an age.

Eventually, a taxi arrived, I lifted my suitcase into the boot, and we sped toward my new school. A few minutes later, we drove through the entrance to Brooke House College, a grand, ivy-covered Georgian mansion where the headmaster, Mr. Donald Williams, and his wife, Joan, were there to welcome me. At the turn of the twentieth century, this building had served as a winter hunting lodge for a distinguished old English family—the de Capell Brookes—and all those years later, it still retained its warm, high-spirited, collegial atmosphere.[13]

But for all its old-world charms, the school was relatively new, and it focused on helping international students switch to the British education system. My father liked the school when he had visited the previous year, and he liked the fact that it took boarders: he thought that this would keep me in check and help me focus on my studies.

As things turned out, he could not have been more wrong.

* * *

On that first exciting day, I was shown to my boarding house, where I shared a room with a young white Rhodesian—Zimbabwe would not win independence from Britain for another seven years. I was then taken to the hall, where we were treated to a sumptuous meal. It was a propitious beginning. But ultimately, my time in England was marred by underachievement, although it was no less formative for that. I studied four A-levels: mathematics, chemistry, physics and biology. I had graduated with distinction in Kuwait, and so my ambition was to win a place to study medicine at university.

But once in England, far from home, living on my own, I had my head turned: by girls, by smoking and drinking and by the extraordinary events happening back home. A few weeks after my arrival, the third Arab-Israeli war, sometimes known as the Yom Kippur War, erupted: Egypt's leader, Anwar Sadat, promised that the PLO would be handed control of the West Bank and Gaza, if Israel were defeated.

Israel won the war and retained control of the Palestinian territories, including Halhul and the rest of the West Bank. But the Arab world retaliated, imposing an oil embargo on countries that supported Israel, including Britain. By January 1974, the British government had imposed a three-day work week, as it tried to conserve dwindling energy resources by reducing the consumption of electricity produced by coal-burning power stations.

At Brooke House, we had to get used to routine power cuts, when we occasionally had to resort to using candles to see anything.

And I remember once walking round Piccadilly Circus—London's answer to New York's Times Square—and noticing how all the buildings no longer had their iconic, flashing neon lights.

Eventually, the oil embargo was lifted, and the spirits of every Palestinian were lifted by some thrilling news from the United Nations in New York. In November 1974, as I began the second year of my A-levels, the young, dashing leader of the PLO, Yasser Arafat, delivered a now-famous speech at the UN assembly. Wearing his trademark black-and-white *keffiyeh*, and donning dark shades, which he took off as he ramped up the rhetoric, Mr. Arafat said, "Today I have come bearing an olive branch and a freedom-fighter's gun. Do not let the olive branch fall from my hand. I repeat: do not let the olive branch fall from my hand."[14] Nine days later, the UN reaffirmed the inalienable rights of the Palestinian people to self-determination, national independence and sovereignty, and the right of the Palestinians to return to their homes and property.[15]

This was a hugely exciting time, and strangely ironic: my father had been studying in England as Palestine was being erased from the map, and now I was studying in England as Palestine seemed to be on the cusp of independence. Throughout this period, I became heavily engaged in lively political debates, and I was an active member of the General Union of Palestinian Students, which was affiliated to the PLO. During the school holidays, I often traveled down to London to spend time with my Palestinian friends, and we would dream of returning to our lost homeland.

It was while I was on one of these trips that I realized that I was the only one among my friends who went to a private boarding school. So, for my second year, I moved to another school: Kettering Technical College. Although it was only about twenty miles from Brooke House College, it was a world away in terms of academics and atmosphere. It was a state-run institution, housed in a perfunctory, redbrick building.[16] But it felt right, for all that.

Looking back, it was a blatant act of rebellion—my first, when I think about it. Until then, I had spent my life in my father's shadow. I recall once visiting the home of his beloved former landlady, a feisty woman called Molly Tell, who had clearly adored my father when he was studying in Leeds. It was she who had enthused my father with socialist ideas, and they stayed in touch. When I paid her a visit, she was well into her seventies, but she was still very active, and actually came to pick me up at the Leeds train station in her little Morris Minor. I stayed with her for a few days, and I enjoyed my time, taking the opportunity to tour the Lake District and the Yorkshire Dales. But she could not stop reminiscing about my father, and I never came out well when she made a comparison, as she often did.

"You look like a spoiled kid," she told me once, after seeing me light up a cigarette. "Your father wasn't. He was a very hard worker. He used to study all the time. He barely left the room during the day."

When I retorted "I'm bored," she fired back with a scalding remark.

"How can an eighteen-year-old boy be bored when there are so many books to read and so many things to be done in life?"

She had a point, and I am ashamed to say that her comments fell on deaf ears. But if I thought that I could escape my father's shadow, I could not escape his scrutiny. He was not happy about my decision to leave Brooke House College—and that's putting it mildly. Perhaps if my grades had been better, he might just have accepted my move to Kettering. But they weren't, so he didn't. Things came to a head one day when I heard a knock on the door of the apartment where I was now staying. Rather sleepily, I went to open the door. As I pulled it back, I was given the shock of my life. There, standing on the doorstep, was my father.

Without telling me, he had traveled the three thousand miles from Kuwait, and he had arranged an interview with the headmaster, an austere and no-nonsense Scot called James McKinlay. That meeting was a catastrophe. Mr. McKinlay was unflinching in his criticism of me: I was not a good student, I did not turn up for lessons, my grades were poor.

After we left the headmaster's office, I pleaded with my father for a second chance. I promised that I would work hard and that things would work out. He agreed to let me stay on so that I could complete my A-levels. He was like the football referee who holds up a yellow card.

I really did work hard in the last few months of the academic year. I had a new goal in sight: to study engineering at one of three universities: Manchester, Nottingham or Warwick. But after all my wayward activities, I just had too much ground to make up, and when I got my A-level results, I failed to get the As and Bs I needed for entry to university. When I phoned home with the news, I begged my father for one more chance. But he said, "No. Enough is enough. Come home and we will talk about it here." That was his way of giving me a red card, although I would not know the full extent of his anger and disappointment for a few more days.

When I flew home to Kuwait, I was greeted by my mother. But my father refused to see me. Eventually, after two days, I was summoned to his office in the city. There, he ran one of Kuwait's biggest law practices, with fifty partners and a long list of prestigious clients. I arrived at the appointed time, but my father forced me to wait outside his office. Finally, I was asked to enter the room. I saw him sitting at his desk on the far side, scribbling away—there were no computers back then. He looked every bit the smart, successful barrister that he was. I tried to attract his attention. But he did not look up. He made no attempt to acknowledge the fact that I was there.

After several minutes, he stopped writing, took off his spectacles, placed them down on the desk in a very slow and deliberate manner, and looked at me. He started talking. He spoke softly, but there was a simmering anger that let me know how disappointed he was.

As he finished, I became aware of two brown envelopes on the desk in front of him. One was large, bulging with something. The other appeared empty. He saw me looking at them, and he then began to explain what they were.

"This envelope contains the money that I have saved for your higher education in England," he said. "But I am sorry to say that you will not have any of it because you do not deserve to have any of it." As the enormity of what he was saying started to sink in, he passed me the second envelope. "Take this," he said. Inside, I found bank notes amounting to a paltry two hundred dollars. "From now on, you will have to manage everything yourself."

With those few brutal words, he broke the umbilical cord. I got up, turned round and left his office. Looking back, I fully appreciate the wisdom of my father's actions. If he had bailed me out, I may never have learned to find my own way in the world—and I am certain that I would not have become an entrepreneur.

But at the time, I felt bruised, confused and alone.

* * *

Within a few days, I was on a plane to Damascus. I traveled to the Syrian capital at my mother's suggestion. There, I could stay with one of her sisters, free of charge, while I sorted out my life. Until she passed away in 2012, my mother was the peacemaker of the family, smoothing the way and working tirelessly in the background to make things work. Time and time again, her extraordinary family network—she had brothers and sisters, uncles and aunts, and cousins living everywhere—came to the rescue. It was her brother who helped my father find a job in Kuwait after the disaster of the Six-Day War in 1967. It was her uncle I stayed with in England when I first arrived in the country. And now it was her sister who provided me with some shelter during that torrid time.

If free board and lodging was one of the big reasons why I went to Damascus, it was not the only reason. The other reason was to win a scholarship to study abroad. While I was in England, I discovered that many of my Palestinian friends had received funding from the PLO, which set aside funds to create an educated professional class who would be ready to build a new Palestinian nation when the time came. In Damascus, the PLO's education division was offering scholarships to students who wished to study in Eastern Europe. At first, I dreamed of studying in East Germany, which was renowned for its engineering prowess. Every day, I called the PLO's student office, and I was given every indication that I would be given a scholarship to study there. But each time I called, I was told that no decision had been made. "Call back tomorrow," they said.

In the end, I was forced to make a decision, for reasons very far from educational. One day, my uncle, who was a brilliant engineer and served in the United Nations' Food and Agriculture Organization, asked me, with a glint in his eye, "Are you going to be staying here for long?" You see, he had five daughters, and he was on the lookout for five sons-in-law. Rightly or wrongly, I suddenly feared that I would be forced into an arranged marriage with one of my cousins.

The next day, I called the student office. They still had no news about my hoped-for scholarship to East Germany. They must have sensed my disappointment because the scholarship officer then said, "But we do have a scholarship for a place at a university in Bulgaria." She might as well have said "the Moon." I really had no idea where Bulgaria was. If you have ever seen *The Last King of Scotland*, where the young Scottish doctor played by

James McAvoy chooses where to travel by sticking a pin in the map and ending up in Idi Amin's Uganda, you will know something of my feelings at that moment.

But by then, I really had no other option. I said, "Yes, I'll take it."

Within a few weeks, I was flying to Sofia, Bulgaria's capital, where I was to spend the next five years.

Chapter 3

BEHIND THE
IRON CURTAIN

I VIVIDLY REMEMBER THE MOMENT THE AIRPLANE FROM Damascus touched down at the airport at Sofia, the tires screeching as they hit the tarmac. I remember thinking that I was embarking on a new chapter in my life—and I was excited, if a little apprehensive.

Just before landing, when the airplane was making its descent, I had looked out of the tiny cabin window, and I was struck by how rural the country was. It was September—harvest time—and the whole landscape was scattered with farms and fields and was glazed by a golden autumnal hue as far as the eye could see.

It augured well, I thought.

But that thought did not last long. No sooner had I stepped off the plane than I was being hurried through the airport terminal, where I was confronted by a cacophony of unfamiliar sounds and a dizzying array of signs in the Cyrillic script of Bulgaria's Slavic language. I wondered how on earth I would ever be able to learn this strange foreign tongue, with its back-to-front letters and upside-down words.

I managed to navigate my way through passport control. And then came my next challenge: How was I going to get to my halls of residence? Fortunately, on the two-hour flight from Damascus, I had befriended some fellow students who were returning after the summer holidays. They were already fluent in Bulgarian, and they kindly put me in a taxi and told the driver where I needed to go.

As I journeyed to the university, I had some time to reflect on my impulsive decision to take the scholarship in Bulgaria. What an extraordinary turn of events! Barely one month earlier, I had been sweating my A-level results in England, wondering if I would soon be heading to a *British* university. Now, I was heading to a *Bulgarian* university, having been awarded a generous scholarship by the PLO. Little did I know then that I would be completely transformed by the experience, that I would undergo—perhaps "endure" is a better word—a process of gradual, and sometimes painful, change.

But if my personal transformation was gradual—I arrived in 1975 and did not leave until 1980—my awakening was instant. Now, more than forty years later, I can still recall the moment when everything changed. I was sitting on the edge of a lumpy, uncomfortable, metal-framed bed, staring at the four plain walls of the room that would be my home for the next year. Minutes earlier, the airport taxi had dropped me outside the grim, grey, concrete university hostel, and I had been shown to the room. As I was the first student to arrive, I was given a choice of the four beds in the room. It was not much of a choice.

For the first time in my life, I felt cornered. I literally had nowhere else to go. My father had all but washed his hands of me. And now I was here, behind the Iron Curtain, in a Communist country I knew nothing about, with a language I couldn't speak. For a split second, life looked bleak. For a split second, I wanted to turn back the clock.

I might have crumbled. But on that day, in that room far from home, in that moment of desperation, I resolved to change my ways.

I think the turning point was when a story that I had first heard during my school days came rushing back into my thoughts. It was an epiphany, of sorts. As you can imagine, my mind was racing, thinking through my options, and it was then that I recalled the heroics of the great Arab leader, Tariq Ibn Ziyad. In 711, he led an army of seven thousand soldiers across the narrow strait separating North Africa and Europe and landed beneath the sharply rising hill that now bears his name: the Rock of Gibraltar, the Spanish corruption of the Arabic *Jabal Tariq*, or "mountain of Tariq." His task was to conquer territory controlled by the Visigoths, the previously all-conquering Germanic people who had sacked Rome three hundred years earlier—an event widely considered to mark the end of the Roman Empire in the West. There were many doubters among Tariq's army. Some wanted to return home. Some threatened to mutiny. To prevent this, he took what, on the face of it, looks like a reckless, suicidal act. He ordered all his boats to be burned. As a result, retreat was not an option.

With no alternative but to fight, Tariq's troops proved to be a formidable foe. Over the next seven years, the Arab forces seized control of a vast swathe of the Iberian Peninsula.

As I sat on the bed, I realized that I, too, had burned all my boats, although I readily admit that I had done so without any deliberate, strategic focus. I had squandered the opportunities that had come my way. And now there was only one viable course of action.

I had to stop making excuses. I had to learn the language. I had to get my degree.

I had to stand on my own two feet.

* * *

In 1975, Bulgaria was still largely closed to the outside world. Ever since the Second World War, it had been closely allied with the Soviet Union, and it was run by one party: the Bulgarian Communist Party. I was able to go there because the PLO, which by then had become the accepted formal representative of the dispersed Palestinian people, had only recently forged a new relationship with a variety of countries in the Soviet bloc. As part of efforts to build on the momentum that followed Yasser Arafat's famous speech to the United Nations, the PLO resolved to expand its presence in Eastern Europe, where it only had representative offices in East Germany, Romania and Yugoslavia. It announced plans to staff new offices in Bulgaria as well as Czechoslovakia, Hungary and Poland.

My scholarship was one of several available as part of an educational collaboration intended to foster closer links between Bulgaria and what was hoped would one day be an independent Palestine. It covered all my tuition and living costs for five years at Bulgaria's elite technical university—then known as the Higher Institute for Mechanical and Electrical Engineering. For three years, I was to study for an undergraduate degree, and then, like my father, I was to carry on for an additional fourth year to complete a master's degree.

But before I could begin my engineering course, I had to pass a tricky hurdle. I had to learn Bulgarian. So, for one whole year, I was put into a multinational, multilingual classroom. There, I began to learn the rudiments of a language spoken by seven million people.

You will know, by now, that I often draw comparisons with Hollywood movies. But here, I will draw a comparison with a British TV comedy, *Mind Your Language!*, from the 1970s. These days, it is rarely rerun, although you can still watch old episodes on YouTube. It tells the story of a young Oxford graduate and his chaotic, confusing, and always amusing encounters with a class of mature foreign students from a variety of different countries who want to learn English. When I first saw the TV program, it took me straight back to my first awkward lessons in the Bulgarian language.

My language class was filled with engineering students who had come to study in Bulgaria from all corners of the globe—including Colombia, the Congo, Cyprus, Mongolia and Vietnam. No one spoke a single word of English, and neither did the teacher. It meant that we had no option but to start speaking Bulgarian. It was the only lingua franca.

From the very first day, we were bombarded with words and pictures, and we had to make connections. And, funnily enough, it worked. Before too long, I had mastered a small group of words and phrases that gave me the freedom to go to the market, meet people for a drink, and generally get around.

I was soon able to travel across the country and see the nation that would be my home for the next five years. It was different than anything I had seen before. There was the language, of course. And the food: I remember my first meal of pea soup, pork stew and damp bread served on a metal plate. (It was a far cry from the welcome dinner I had so enjoyed at my English boarding school.)

There were some familiar things too. I learned, for example, that Bulgaria had once been part of the Ottoman Empire—just like Palestine. In fact, I came to realize that Bulgarian, like Palestinian Arabic, has many words of Turkish origin, a linguistic reminder of a shared history.

But the differences outnumbered the similarities. Perhaps the biggest difference was the system of government: a Communist dictatorship rather than a Capitalist democracy. These days, I am sometimes asked how I could have spent five years behind the Iron Curtain and still ended up as an entrepreneur in a capitalist world?

It is a fair question.

This is my answer. If you really want to be an entrepreneur, you must seek out new experiences, make the most of chance encounters, and start conversations with different people who look at the world in a different way to you. You must be curious, ask questions, and never be satisfied until you truly understand something that was puzzling you. I, of course, did not go to Bulgaria with the express intention of doing this. But when I was there, I could not help but ask questions.

And what did I conclude? In a socialist system, people are given housing, healthcare and jobs—things people have to fight for in a capitalist system. But at the end of the day, every individual is just a number. There is no democracy, no freedom to speak, no freedom to think. If you want to be an entrepreneur, you absolutely need that freedom to speak, freedom to think and freedom to go your own way.

I confess that I went to Bulgaria with some starry-eyed views of socialism. My father, of course, was a great supporter of the broader socialist movement, and he no doubt influenced me. Also, I had read some socialist texts, including Karl Marx's *Communist Manifesto*. But I was disappointed by the way his ideas were hijacked by a narrow elite who ruled as dictators. This is why I never became a convert to communist government during my time in Bulgaria.

I did, however, come to greatly admire the country's first-rate technical education.

* * *

In my first two years, I studied hard, and I did so without the knowledge of my father and mother. When I left Damascus, I did not tell them where I was going, and I only later learned that it was my mother who had instructed my father to mount a search for me. Who knows whether or not I would have ever seen them again if she hadn't taken the initiative? I was making my own way in the world, I was forging my own path, and I was quite happy to do so.

But then, toward the end of the second year, I received a letter in the post. I recognized the handwriting on the envelope. It was from my father. I was totally shocked. This, remember, was long before the internet and Google. In those days, it was much easier to just disappear. He explained how he had looked everywhere for me and how delighted he was that he had now finally tracked me down.

He was friendly—very different to our last exchange—and, as a token of goodwill, he sent me a check for two hundred dollars. It was a welcome gift. Life was hard, money was scarce, and I knew that two hundred dollars would go a long way to easing my situation. I now realize that even then, I was showing signs of the entrepreneur I would become because I was soon on a train to Istanbul five hundred kilometers from Sofia. I had some friends there, and I wanted to cash my father's check for hard currency—not worthless Bulgarian levs.

But if I was glad for the contact—and the cash—I was not sure that I was quite ready to see my father. Indeed, it was another year before I did see him: he, my mother, my two brothers and my sister all came to Bulgaria for a summer holiday. By then, after three years of silence, it was wonderful to be reconciled. My father could see that I had changed. I was no longer the "pampered school boy" living it up in London. Also, I could see that he had changed—he was ready to accept me for who I was.

So, on that memorable visit, we let bygones be bygones and set off on an adventurous trip across Bulgaria, traveling through the Balkan Mountains around Sofia on the western side of the country and stopping at the beaches of the Black Sea on the eastern side.

After my family left for Kuwait, I threw myself into my studies once again, completing my undergraduate degree and embarking on a master's degree on medical electronics, which combined my interests in medicine and engineering. Specifically, I worked on the development of one-channel or single-lead electrocardiographs—more commonly known as ECGs.

The ECG is a critical diagnostic test used for detecting heart problems, such as an arrhythmic pulse that could be a sign of imminent cardiac arrest. Invented in the 1890s by the Dutch physiologist Willem Einthoven, who later won the Nobel Prize for Medicine for this work, the ECG is typically a lengthy, complex, multichannel test. My master's thesis, written in Bulgarian, focused on the one-channel test, which offers patients a quicker readout of their pulse.

It was thrilling to work in such a pioneering, experimental field of medicine. But I did not spend all my time in the engineering laboratory. After four years, I was, as you can imagine, fluent in Bulgarian, and in my final year as an undergraduate, I met and married my Bulgarian girlfriend (those first, halting steps in the language, taken when I first arrived in the country, were a distant memory). Then, a year later, just before graduation, I became a father for the first time, at the age of twenty-four. We named our son Amir—"prince" in Arabic but also in Slavic, where it more commonly appears as Vladimir, or "renowned prince."

My son's arrival capped an extraordinary period for me. Who could have predicted the course of events when my plane landed five years earlier? Not me, that's for sure. Nowadays, when I am asked what I picked up during my time in Bulgaria, I sometimes make a joke: "I went with nothing," I say, "and came back with three certificates: a degree certificate, a marriage certificate and a birth certificate." But, in fact, I came back with a fourth thing too—not another certificate but a philosophy of life that I have tried to follow ever since.

During my five years in Bulgaria, I learned, little by little, to adapt to the new environment. I learned to get stronger. Looking back, there was something brutally Darwinian about the process of personal transformation. I'm now inclined to think that everyone—certainly every entrepreneur—must have their own version of my formative "Bulgarian moment" when they are pushed to the limit. That's because, throughout our lives, we all face many such make-or-break tests, so the sooner we learn how to deal with them, the better.

Of course, the process of change is not something you undertake in a particularly conscious way. You adapt or you don't. That's it.

But in the years since then, I have tried to rationalize what I did. Why did I adapt? Why did I come through my first big test? What were the factors that helped me thrive?

I have thought long and hard about these questions. And now, I attribute my success in Bulgaria to three traits—all of which, I believe, are critical characteristics of the entrepreneur. First, I was *diverse*. That meant I was open to new things, I was ready and willing to broaden my horizons, and specifically I was eager to learn a new language and culture. Second, I was *dynamic*. That meant I devoted a considerable amount of time and energy to whatever I was doing. I worked hard and I stayed focused. Third, I was *distinctive*, or at least I tried to be. That meant I not only had to work hard, but I also had to excel in whatever I was doing if I was going to stand out in a crowd.

These three words—diverse, dynamic, distinctive—have become a kind of mantra for me. Whenever I am in a challenging situation, I ask myself: What do I need to do in order to be diverse, dynamic and distinctive? Invariably, my attempt to answer the question helps me come to a good solution.

* * *

There is one particularly memorable episode when, with hindsight, I now realize that I exhibited all three of these entrepreneurial traits.

Toward the end of my time in Bulgaria, I paid a visit to see my family in Kuwait. By then, my relations with my father had begun to thaw. He was content to welcome me home again because he could see that I was trying to get back on track (although he was unhappy about my marriage, which took place without his express permission).

During that visit, I bumped into an old friend who, it turned out, was looking to buy some forklift trucks for his employer. In one of those strange quirks of fate, I had recently befriended a fellow student who was working in a Bulgarian factory that was making forklift trucks under license from Bosch, the German engineering company. When I told my Kuwaiti friend about my new acquaintance, he looked skeptical. "Who would want to buy a Bulgarian forklift truck?" he said, dismissively. But when I informed him that the vehicles were German-designed and a fifth of the price of German-made trucks, he changed his tune.

To cut a long story short, I brokered a deal between my two friends and took a commission of four thousand dollars. In doing so, I proved to myself that I could be diverse, dynamic and distinctive: although I was studying medical electronics, I was constantly looking to broaden my knowledge, connections and acquaintances, and seize unique opportunities.

The German-designed, Bulgarian-made forklift truck was my first taste of entrepreneurial deal-making. It took me back to the time I spent with my grandmother in the bazaars of Jerusalem, where I watched her haggle and strike bargains.

And it whetted my appetite for more.

Chapter 4

MY FIRST BUSINESS

On a sweltering Saturday in September 1980, I was sitting in a stuffy room in a Kuwaiti hospital reading through a tedious technical manual about cardiac catheterization—the invasive procedure for diagnosing and treating heart conditions. Three days earlier, I had flown back from Bulgaria after completing my studies, and while I briefly dreamed of starting my own business after the success of my forklift truck venture, the practical reality of needing to support a family drove me to accept the offer of a job as a service engineer for Siemens, the German industrial giant.

So there I was, in the hospital, minding my own business, when all of a sudden, the lights went out. There had been a power cut. Then, I heard the rushing sound of nurses running through the darkened corridors, shouting something. I vaguely heard the words "Siemens engineer." Seconds later, a nurse burst into the room where I was reading and said, "Come quickly, you're needed in the operating room."

I jumped up, put my heavy tome to one side and followed the nurse. When I got to the operating theater, I found a group of anxious doctors and a man lying on the operating table, awaiting surgery. By this time, power had been restored and the lights were back on, but the catheter machine was not working, and the surgeon was unable to continue with the delicate heart operation.

I opened the cabinet containing the catheter machine. I wondered whether the machine had simply fused. I fiddled with the plugs and flicked a few switches. Nothing worked. As time passed, I looked behind me, and saw that all the doctors had crowded around me, watching my every move.

After what seemed like an age—although it was probably only five minutes—the doctors lost patience and hurried the patient to another operating theater. I was left feeling embarrassed. I realize now that I should probably have been better trained. I was just a rookie and I was thrown into an impossible situation on day one. But I did learn an important lesson that day. Never again would I start a job without doing the proper preparation, without knowing my stuff. Never again would I be anything but disciplined, wholly committed to whatever I was doing, and totally responsible for my actions.

I also learned about something else: the central, and growing, importance of computer software. If computers drove the catheter machine, it was software that drove the computers. If this seems blindingly obvious today, it didn't back then. And it was this revelation that caused me to get on a plane and fly to Orlando in Florida.

* * *

In 1982, after two years at Siemens in Kuwait, I jumped at the chance to join Technology International Corporation, a US firm headquartered in the Sunshine State. It was founded by Khaled Diab, a Palestinian who had taken American citizenship after being forced to flee his homeland during the *Nakba* of 1948. He studied for his doctorate in electrical engineering at the University of Iowa and worked for several companies, including Westinghouse Electric Corporation, before establishing his own business.

Specializing in Arabic-English word processors, TIC was part of an extraordinary technological ecosystem based around two main centers: NASA, the American space agency, and Disney, the media and entertainment conglomerate. Today, Silicon Valley is the undisputed leader of the world's computer industry. But back then, Orlando offered a very competitive alternative. When I first stepped off the plane at Orlando Airport, having traveled more than seven thousand miles from Kuwait (arriving via New York), I felt as if I had been transported far into the future. My days in Bulgaria, living behind the Communist Iron Curtain, seemed a long time ago. Here, in the self-proclaimed "land of the free," I relished the mind-expanding, liberating environment. Everything seemed to be moving with lightning speed. NASA had just launched the first of its pioneering there-and-back shuttle missions, when Columbia took off from the nearby Kennedy Space Center at Cape Canaveral. And, as I was getting used to my new surroundings, Disney unveiled its futuristic EPCOT theme park in Orlando, complete with whiz-bang computers that boasted touch screens, 3D imaging, and other wacky features.

My day job back then was helping TIC develop Arabic-English software. Dr. Diab owned a patent for creating software that enabled the authentic representation of Arabic lettering on a computer. It was based on a mathematical formula that overcomes the problem that every Arabic letter has a different shape, or glyph, according to its place in a word. In the course of my work, I came to understand about two remarkable trends that would have an enduring impact on my life. One was the *miniaturization* of computers. It was Gordon Moore, Intel's founder-genius, who back in 1965 predicted that the number of transistors on a microchip (and therefore its speed and capability) would double every two years—a prediction that has since been enshrined as "Moore's Law." And in the early 1980s, I saw this happening with my own eyes. I recall the first time I looked at an IBM personal computer, which had been launched the year before my arrival in the United States: it was a thing of wonder. Inside, it had Intel's 8088 microprocessor (which squeezed 29,000 transistors on a single integrated circuit, up from 2,250 on Intel's first microprocessor) and Microsoft's MS-DOS operating system.

Of course, the miniaturization trend continues unabated: it is said that the latest Apple iPhone is vastly more powerful than the huge computer that guided Neil Armstrong's Apollo 11 mission to the Moon in 1969. But it was the second trend that really influenced me and shaped my thinking: the *democratization* of computers. With the PC, computers were suddenly affordable, and long-standing retailers such as Sears and Radio Shack, together with the first generation of supermarket-style computer outlets such as Computer Land and Computer City, made them available to the person on the street.

I recall wandering around these cavernous places with a sense of astonishment. They planted in my mind the seeds of a new business idea that I pursued when I returned to Kuwait as TIC's regional manager.

* * *

Back in Kuwait, after an eye-opening year in the United States, I started thinking about setting up a Radio Shack-style showroom. But I soon concluded that Kuwait was not the right place to launch this venture. First mover advantage is essential in business, and there were already a number of computer retailers with street-level stores in the emirate.

Where else could I launch the showroom? It did not take me long to decide on Jordan. In some ways, it was not the obvious choice. First, Jordan was, and remains, a relatively poor country, not least because it lacks the natural resources of its richer neighbors. Second, while I had spent more than ten of my formative childhood years in Jordan, I had not been back to the country since we were forced to leave in 1967. If I went back, I would have to resurrect old friendships and make new ones. Third, Jordan did not have a technological ecosystem of the kind I had witnessed in Florida. So I would have to create my own network from scratch. Yet, despite these drawbacks, Jordan did have a lot going for it. In particular, it boasted a relatively well-educated population and, importantly, there was no street-level computer store anywhere in the country.

Having weighed up the pros and cons, I decided to take the gamble of my life and board a plane to Amman. Within a few months, I was the proud owner of a computer showroom in the city's new Tel A'a Ali district and the founder-CEO of a new company: Jordan Computer Center, otherwise known as JCC. It was my first business.

This opportunity came about after a chance meeting with the six investors behind a software company called Computer & Engineering Bureau (now known as Optimiza Solutions). They were looking to broaden the focus of their business and liked my idea of selling PCs to ordinary consumers—rather than businesses. They put some money into the venture, as did my father, who was now starting to believe in me for the first time in my life. For my part, I invested most of my savings from my time in the United States— enough for me to take a 40 percent stake in the new company.

With the modest startup capital, I had sufficient resources to rent and furnish a brand-new showroom. But there was a snag. I did not have enough money to stock the showroom with computers. So, thinking laterally, I approached all the resellers of the big computer brands operating in Jordan and invited them to send me a consignment of their bestselling computers to stock in my showroom. In return, I told them, I would take a commission. In a sense, the Jordan Computer Center was a brick-and-mortar version of the Amazon model—ten years before Jeff Bezos started his online bookstore.

The resellers agreed, with surprising speed. Typically, they were located in dreary, featureless, corporate offices, and they put very little effort into the marketing of the computers, which were mainly sold to big businesses. I offered them a chance to showcase their products in an attractive setting and reach a new group of consumers. After my experience in the United States, I had become a firm believer in the idea that consumers should be able to "try before they buy." I promised the resellers that my showroom would be an exciting venue where consumers could drop in, browse at their leisure, play with the various computers and associated gadgets, and imagine they were the owners.

I stocked all kinds of computer brands—hallowed names from the first age of the PC which have now either been consigned to the history books or which have long since stopped manufacturing PCs. For example, there was Atari, which now only makes video games. There was Commodore, which is now defunct. There was Sinclair, which still exists but no longer makes PCs. And there was Texas Instruments, which created the world's first sixteen-bit home computer, but which now focuses on manufacturing components for computers.

From the start, my showroom attracted a steady flow of customers through the door. But it was hard work. The prices were relatively high because electronic goods carried customs duties. Every day, I faced an uphill battle to convert consumer interest into a sale. I did, however, try to remain optimistic, and I was delighted to see that parents and their children—not only wealthy businesspeople—came to the showroom. That confirmed my opinion that Jordanians were prepared to invest significantly in their children's education. Taking heart from this, I resolved to put even more effort into my enterprise as I approached the first anniversary of my showroom's opening.

It was then that I got some devastating news. I was browsing through the newspaper when I came across a story about a new

Jordanian company that had just won the lucrative contract to stock the brand-new IBM PCs in a showroom. As I read to the end of the story, the news got worse. It transpired that it was *my fellow investors,* people I considered my friends and partners, who were behind the new company. In other words, as I saw it then, they had gone behind my back, cut me out of a deal with IBM, and set up a rival showroom.

I felt totally betrayed, and on the advice of my father, I hired a lawyer. Happily, the dispute was resolved to my satisfaction: I was free to buy out the other investors. But it was not clear what I could do next. I could not keep the showroom in the Tel A'a Ali district because it was located in the same building as the offices of the investors' company. Also, given that my rivals were going to be selling IBMs—the best PCs in the world—I knew I would struggle to compete if I continued to sell Ataris, Commodores and Sinclairs. So I started searching for a new location for my showroom *and* a new business idea.

Almost straightaway, I found the new location in Shmeisani—a buzzing, youthful, entrepreneurial district in the heart of Amman. But it took a bit longer to find the new business idea.

The breakthrough came when I heard about a Kuwaiti technology company that had just struck a deal with Microsoft Corporation.

* * *

It was 1985, and while Microsoft was not yet the world-beating company it is today, it was still regarded as one of the rising stars of the global computing industry. So when Sakhr Software Company, a division of Al Alamiah Group, won the contract to produce the first Arabic MSX computer, it was big news across the Middle East. Manufactured by Yamaha in Japan, the MSX was a special, affordable home computer that Microsoft produced for markets in Asia, the Gulf countries and the rest of the Middle East. Simple to use, it was more a console than a computer, and it could be plugged into a TV. The Sakhr MSX, customized with an Arabic keyboard, provided the platform for a rich blend of education and entertainment—"edutainment," as it's sometimes called—and thousands of Arab children learned English, math and other subjects through Sakhr's educational video games.

I was immediately attracted by what Sakhr was doing—in particular, the Arabic-English specialization together with the focus on edutainment software. With my background in Arabic-English software, and my understanding of the family edutainment market, I felt I would make the perfect reseller in Jordan. All I had to do was convince the company's owner.

That was not going to be so easy. For a start, Mohammed Al-Sharekh was, and remains, one of Kuwait's top businessmen. Back then, he was in his early forties, he already had a distinguished career as a banker and economist behind him, having served as the deputy director of the Kuwait Fund for Economic Development (1969–1973), the deputy executive director of the International Bank for Reconstruction and Development in Washington (1973–1975), and the chairman of the board of directors of Kuwait Industrial Bank (1975–1979). After stepping down from this last role, he established the Al-Alamiah Group and launched the software division in 1982, taking the name "Sakhr"—which means "rock" in Arabic. His deal with Bill Gates, Microsoft's co-founder, was something of a corporate coup and catapulted Al-Sharekh to greater prominence in the region. So, why would he bother taking time out of his busy schedule to meet me?[17]

Another problem was tracking him down. This, remember, was long before LinkedIn and the possibility of texting a potential contact or sending a quick speculative email. I asked around, raided my network of contacts in Kuwait, and remained hopeful until I eventually found a friend who personally knew Al-Sharekh. I asked him if he would introduce me. Yes, he said. Even so, it took several weeks of persistent calling before Al-Sharekh agreed to see me.

When I finally got to meet him, I quickly realized that convincing him to give me some of his business was going to be an uphill struggle. Educated in Egypt and the United States, he is formidably intelligent, but he does not suffer fools gladly, and he can be abrupt and abrasive. As soon as we sat down to talk, he started firing a barrage of questions at me: Who are you? Why are you here? Why should I give you a reseller's contract? He then asked me to prepare him a feasibility study. I thought I would be given a few days to put this together—but no. He showed me to a little room with a computer and asked me to work there and submit the report on Microsoft Multiplan—the Excel spreadsheet of its day. Not only that, but he stood behind me, watching what I did. It was clear he wanted to see how I would perform under pressure. He kept me on my toes.

Thankfully, he seemed impressed with my report. But he was not yet ready to take me on as a partner. It was only after another few meetings, held several weeks apart and involving several back-and-forth trips between Amman and Kuwait, that I was finally awarded the contract to sell Sakhr computers in Jordan.

In the end, my persistence was rewarded. At the time, I jumped for joy. My old consignment business was falling apart. So, if I hadn't managed to strike the deal with Al-Sharekh, my business may have gone under. But now, all these years later, I realize the deal was not just about survival. It paved the way for a period of sustained success as an entrepreneur—when I built up the business, built up my finances and built up my confidence.

After signing the agreement, I returned to Jordan and got to work. Right from the start, and as I wrote in my feasibility report, I was convinced that Jordanians—given their commitment of education—would buy the Sakhr MSX computers.

I was right.

They flew out of the store. Indeed, over the next five years, I sold no fewer than ten thousand MSX computers, which were primarily designed for the children's market. In those days, there was no how-to guide for entrepreneurs—at least, not in Jordan. I just tried different things and waited to see what worked. I opened two more of my own stores (in addition to my main showroom in Shmeisani), I signed agreements with computer dealers in other Jordanian cities, I loaned equipment to schools and colleges where the teachers became my representatives, I made arrangements with the Housing Bank for Trade and Finance so that parents could use their mortgage or other savings as collateral when buying the computers by installments, and I marketed the computers through a series of training events and academic conferences.

You might think that these computers were the preserve of wealthy parents and their children. But actually, all kinds of people bought them. They really were a democratizing force. I vividly recall watching a street cleaner, dressed in his yellow high-vis overalls, standing outside the showroom and looking in the window. Next thing, he was opening the door and walking toward me. "I want to buy a computer for my kid," he said. It was the beginning of the month, and he had just been paid. He proceeded to hand me his entire monthly salary. Like so many Jordanians, he wanted his child to have a very different life than his own, and he believed that computers could help.

But if my hunch that Jordanians would love Sakhr's Arabic computers was right, I was wrong about something else. As I will explain in the next chapter, I underestimated the importance of building a diversified business.

Chapter 5

THE FIRST GULF WAR, BANKRUPTCY & SURVIVAL

THROUGHOUT MY FIRST SIX YEARS AS A BUSINESS OWNER, I WAS advised to expand—to new products and new markets beyond Jordan. "Diversify! Diversify!" my closest friends told me. "You never know what's around the corner." They warned me that home computers would be subject to a bell curve, like any other product: just as sales had risen, they would eventually fall.

But I'm afraid to say that, with the confidence of the brash young man that I was, I ignored them, convinced that since my business was going well, there was no reason to think that it wouldn't continue to do so. Bell curves? Why do they apply to me? Hadn't I just sold ten thousand computers? Hadn't I just organized a regional conference under the patronage of Prince Hassan bin Talal, Crown Prince of Jordan and brother of the King?

That attitude proved disastrous for me. It blinded me to the fact that, for all my undoubted success, I was, as a reseller of other people's goods, no more than a follower. I did not realize that, if you are to succeed as an entrepreneur, you need to be a leader, not a follower.

Looking back, with the benefit of hindsight, I realize that I was heading for a fall. The price of personal computers was tumbling—as a result of the growing prevalence of China and Taiwan's manufacturing prowess and the ingenuity of Intel, which was following the famous law of its founder, Gordon Moore, and growing exponentially. But every corporate cataclysm needs a trigger event, and mine was the first Gulf War.

I remember the first day like it was yesterday: Thursday, August 2, 1990. That was when the world woke up to the news that the Iraqi ruler, Saddam Hussein, had launched an invasion of Kuwait. I switched on the TV, and as I watched the pictures of tanks rolling over the border, I knew there and then that my business would all but collapse.

And so it proved true.

In those days, companies did not typically have sophisticated resilience plans or disaster recovery centers. So when Saddam's soldiers invaded Kuwait, destroying everything in their path, Mohammed Al-Sharekh's Al Alamiah Group, which was based in the emirate, was forced to abandon production of the Sakhr computers I sold to Jordanians.

For a while, Al-Sharekh and I tried to keep the business afloat. Together, we worked on survival strategies. For instance, some of his software engineers came to Jordan, and we hoped they could keep on working. But in the end, we saw that the writing was on the wall. As the US Navy's blockade of the Jordanian port of Aqaba (intended to stop the traffic of oil, food and other supplies to Saddam's Iraq) started to have a wider economic impact, we knew that we would struggle to carry on. When reality dawned, Al-Sharekh left for Saudi Arabia and moved his Sakhr business to Cairo in Egypt. Never again did Sakhr produce computers. I, for my part, was left with thousands of unsold computers, and I was plunged into debt amounting to $1.5 million.

As I stared down the black hole of bankruptcy, I resolved that there was no future for me in Jordan. I concluded that I must start again. Like many Jordanians and Kuwaitis, I decided to try my luck in Canada. I applied to the immigration authorities, and I was awarded the right to settle in a place I'd never heard of and could barely pronounce: Saskatchewan.

In some ways, it was like going to Bulgaria all over again.

I flew to Montreal, leaving behind my wife and daughter, who were set to join me once I had found a place to live.

It was winter, and the temperature was −14°C. Although my family came from the Hebron Mountains, this Canadian cold was almost unbearable. I then traveled on to Toronto, where it was even icier. There, I briefly met up with my brother, Raed—or Ray, as we call him. He had already left Kuwait, having decided within a few weeks of Saddam's invasion that there was no future for him there. A graduate of the University of Central Florida, he found it easy to acclimatize to his new environment, and he has remained in North America ever since, having taking Canadian and US citizenship.

After Toronto, I moved on to Vancouver, staying in lodgings recommended by my expatriate friends. A relatively warm and stunningly beautiful place on the Pacific coast of British Columbia, it had a distinct feel of the old country I remembered from my time at school in England, with its quaint manners and civilized feel.

But however bright the sky, there was a heavy gloom that hung in the air. There was real fear about Saddam's supposed weapons of mass destruction, and my fellow Jordanian-Kuwaiti exiles struggled to come to terms with their losses. I had come to the New World for a fresh start, but I felt weighed down by these burdens. The optimism I sought was nowhere to be found.

Things came to a head on February 22, 1991. On that day, President Bush gave Saddam Hussein a twenty-four-hour ultimatum: get out of Kuwait or get ready to face the full wrath of the US Army's ground troops. It was an extraordinary turn of events. I had barely been in Canada for one month, and suddenly there was a glimmer of hope that Kuwait would be liberated. It was then that I realized I needed to return home—I needed to be with my family. Of course, I had been an exile many times over. But I now felt the pain of the vast distance separating me from my loved ones. Canada, I concluded, was not my place. So I made the return journey to Jordan.

I never got to see Saskatchewan.

* * *

Back home in Amman, I found a very different place to the one I had left only a few months before. In the aftermath of Iraq's invasion of Kuwait, Jordan had seen an influx of people, mainly Jordanian Palestinians, from Kuwait. Generally, these were not refugees but "returnees"—people who had left Palestine in the late 1940s or Jordan in the late 1960s. In all, some 300,000 émigrés poured back into Jordan, increasing the country's population by 10 percent.

Where those in Canada had been overwhelmed by a sense of gloom, those returning to Jordan were altogether more opti-mistic—in spite of the serious geopolitical environment. Many of them were doctors, engineers, lawyers, financiers—profes-sional, educated people who wanted to rebuild their lives and their businesses. My father, who was head of a committee that raised funds for the 35 percent of returnees who were in "dire need," told the *New York Times* that of the rest, 10 percent were "well off" and another 55 percent were able to draw on funds in Kuwaiti bank accounts.[18]

I met up with several of these returnees. Some were old school friends who were looking to make a go of it in the land of their birth. Others were people I knew through my collaboration with Mohammed Al-Sharekh—notably Fahed Abu Higleh, who had worked for Sakhr and joined me as commercial manager. Now a partner in the firm, serving as chief sales officer, he has been with me through thick and thin all these years. Together, the returnees helped me to think afresh about my business. We asked ourselves a series of questions: Which industry or sector is fast-moving? Which can generate money? Which is open to new ideas?

To guide me further, I also sought the advice of an ex-EY consul-tant. He gave me two critical pieces of advice. First, he said, "Sell your stock of Sakhr computers, even if you have to dump them at half price." This I did, and I was pleased I did so when I did, because they were soon worth less than the price I sold them for. Second, he said, "Shift your focus from B2C [business-to-consumer] to B2B [business-to-business] and specialize not on reselling computers and other products but on providing services and solutions." This I also did, although getting started was by no means easy.

As soon as I had offloaded my old computer stock, I was able to reschedule my debt payments with several banks. I have learned over the years that bankers are not really the friends of the entrepreneur. They are only too willing to give you an umbrella when it is sunny and only too willing to take it away when it starts to rain. They are a practical necessity for new businesses, but their veins are filled with ice-cold blood, and I vowed that as soon as I could turn to other forms of finance, I would.

In those difficult times, I was lucky that my father was willing to stand as the ultimate guarantor for my huge $1.5 million debt. The banks nevertheless offered me extortionate rates of interest. But what alternative did I have? None. I therefore had to try every which way to reduce the mountain of debt and, ultimately, pay back the loan. It meant trying out a variety of business ideas. In a word, it meant *hustling*.

One day, I heard about a government tender issued by the Jordanian Ministry of Education for a project to install computer systems in thirty schools. I thought I had a chance of winning since, through my earlier work with Sakhr, I was known to the ministry. I did indeed make a successful bid, beating a large field of three hundred competitors. This did not solve my financial problems because I had to agree to undertake the work for a low price. On the other hand, it got me noticed, gave my newly recruited staff something to do, and ensured that there was some money coming into the business.

After several months out of business, I was back in the game.

It felt good.

* * *

But the government contract was no more than a stopgap. I had to keep looking for new business opportunities. Perhaps ironically—given that my bank was chasing me to make increasingly egregious interest payments on loans that I had taken out when my business was going well—I started to focus on the banking sector. Some of my returnee friends had taken up jobs in Jordanian banks. They proved a useful source of ideas, insights and intelligence on what kinds of services banks really needed in the new postwar environment.

From my conversations with several of these returnees, it became clear that, amid all the troubles, the banks were *actually expanding*—not shrinking. Among other things, this was because thousands of returnees were starting to receive money from a special compensation fund established by the United Nations for victims of the Gulf War. The recipients of the UN's largesse needed banking services to help them save and invest their money.

It was at this point that I asked the question every entrepreneur should ask themselves when they spot an opportunity: Where do *I* fit into this?

My answer was this: technology. It was clear that the expanding banks needed greater networking capabilities. We therefore experimented with some different networking solutions. Our first business idea focused on satellite connectivity. We were, literally, reaching for the stars. Today, in the era of Starlink, the constellation of satellites being built by Elon Musk's SpaceX company to offer internet access from low earth orbit, satellite connectivity is part of everyday life. Back then, it wasn't.

I dreamed up the satellite idea on the way back from a trip to Hanover, Germany, where I had attended CeBIT, then the world's largest computer industry expo. Essentially, my plan was to create a satellite connectivity business that would link all the banks in Jordan to their customers. To push this forward, I flew to Germany, and I met with key executives from the two companies with the biggest satellite fleets: AT&T and Eutelsat. They liked the idea of breaking into the Jordanian market and agreed to send a delegation of executives to Jordan.

Meanwhile, back in Jordan, I toured the country, visiting every major bank, trying to sell them the idea of satellite connectivity. They agreed not only to meet with the AT&T and Eutelsat's executives but also to invest in a joint venture with me. I arranged the meeting in Jordan, which was conducted under the auspices of Jordan's ministry of technology.

But soon after the meeting, the banks decided to go their own way, forming their own company and striking their own deal with the satellite companies. Frankly, I was devastated. All the time and effort, all the traveling, all the investment (which I could barely afford)—it had come to naught. But I did learn a valuable lesson. If you're going to start a business, you can't just have a bright idea. If you're going to attract investors, you've got to have something more tangible: a product, a market and a team to deliver it all.

I had none of these.

I was definitely wounded by this experience. But I did not look for sympathy. As an entrepreneur, you can't afford to feel sorry for yourself. Like a Formula 1 racing driver who has a crash—you must get straight back into the car.

That's exactly what I did.

Very soon, I was pursuing another business idea—phone banking. If the satellite business failed to get off the launch pad, the phone-banking business really did take off. Indeed, as I will now explain, this business marked a turning point in the fortunes of my company.

* * *

In 1994, I flew to Taiwan, the epicenter of affordable computing. It was part of my constant effort to build my network, make connections, and seek new business ideas. While there, I attended an exhibition, and I met a Taiwanese American who was promoting his voice card-based processing system. We struck up a conversation, and it soon became clear to me that this technology could be applied to Jordan's banking sector. Since the system was founded on a voice card that could be installed on a PC, I realized that it could offer the banks an affordable alternative to the more common, and costly, systems then available to them.

I did a deal with a Taiwanese company: in return for royalty payments, they agreed to show my engineers how their system worked. It seemed a good deal to me. And it was. As soon as I returned home, I sent two of my engineers, Dima Bibi and Yasser Zubaidi, to work side by side with the Taiwanese engineers. Over the next two months, they learned everything about the system, and when they came back to Jordan, we were able to develop the software for a new phone-banking system. As a result, I had been transformed from a reseller to a product provider with my own intellectual property.

With this new software product, I completed another tour of Jordan's banks. This time, I didn't just have a bright idea, I had something tangible to sell. To my delight, we secured a deal to supply the Housing Bank for Trade and Finance, the country's second largest bank, with a new phone-banking system. Again, my old connections came in useful: this was the bank that I worked with when selling the Sakhr computers back in the late 1980s.

We provided the bank with four lines of phone banking and the connectivity to its IBM AS 400 mainframe computer. In doing so, the Housing Bank was the first to offer phone banking in Jordan using the new technology, giving it a competitive edge over its rivals. For my company, JCC, it marked us as one of the rising stars of the nascent Jordanian electronics sector. But it still did not solve my financial problems. To win the contract with the Housing Bank, I had to make a bid that was 40 percent less than my closest rival.

It meant that my search for a truly profitable business had to go on.

* * *

You always have to be on the lookout for business opportunities. In this sense, entrepreneurs can never sleep. They have to be "always on." I know this because my first big breakthrough happened while I was on a family holiday at Limassol in Cyprus in 1996. Actually, I was so strapped for cash that I could not afford to go on holiday. And I could not really afford to take the time off either. But in his own inimitable way, my father persuaded the whole extended family to join him, generously underwriting all the costs.

As things turned out, I found it very hard to switch off. Although my phone-banking business was showing early signs of promise, it did not do much to bring down my mountain of debt. So while it may have looked as though I was relaxing—staring out across the beautiful azure Mediterranean Sea or lounging on a sunbed with a drink in my hand—my mind was elsewhere, thinking about my business.

It was on one such occasion that I was brought abruptly back to the here and now by some shouting coming from the kids' paddling pool, where my daughter, Masa, who was still only a toddler, was playing. To my horror, I became aware that she had slipped over, and she was struggling to get up—that's why people were shouting. I jumped up from my chair, dashed over, scooped her up and held her close. A few minutes later, one of the people sitting by the pool, who had watched the whole drama unfold, came over to see if we were okay.

At first, I was in no mood for polite small talk. I think I must have still been in a state of shock. Yet, for some reason, Colin Warburg persisted. We had England in common, and we soon discovered that we had technology in common too. And before long, we were talking about business. By this time, my daughter had stopped crying and run off to play with one of the extended family, and Colin took the chance to tell me about an opportunity that I soon realized was too good to miss.

It turned out that Warburg's company, Cerberus Software, had developed a PC-based software that linked banks to the Society for Worldwide Interbank Financial Telecommunication—better known as SWIFT.

I knew his software—called NovaSwift—could be game changing in the Middle East.

Back then, most Middle Eastern banks were medium-sized, and they simply could not afford to pay the $500,000 cost of the giant computers used to host the SWIFT technology and which permitted the fast, reliable and safe transfer of money and messages. Instead, they used TELEX, which was altogether slower, clunkier and more cumbersome. If, however, they could access SWIFT technology on a PC, then they would—at last—be able to join an elite club of global banks. Not only that, but they would be able to offer more banking services to a wider group of people, thereby fulfilling one of their core missions: financial inclusion.

Shortly after that fateful conversation in a Cyprus holiday resort, I signed a deal to be a reseller for Cerberus Software—promoting NovaSwift not just in Jordan but also across the rest of the Middle East.

It meant, of course, that I had not managed completely to throw off the label of "reseller." On the other hand, I had, at a stroke, managed to move beyond one product in one market. And very soon, I was serving banks in fourteen countries across the region.

In recognition of this, I determined that it was time to change the name of my company: the Jordanian Computer Centre became Eastern Networks, the forerunner to Eastnets.

Chapter 6
THE RICHEST MAN IN THE WORLD

By 1997, MY BUSINESS WAS GENERATING POSITIVE CASH FLOW, with the success of phone banking and the SWIFT banking business. But I was still massively in debt—to the tune of two million dollars. So I remained on the lookout for new opportunities. Actually, what I really needed was the business version of a winning ticket in a national lottery. Thankfully, toward the end of the year, I found it.

For more than thirty years, from 1957 to 1989, Jordan had been governed by martial law, which severely limited the freedoms of people to go about their business.[19] As I explained in the first chapter, my own father had been a victim of the occasional clampdowns arising from these martial restrictions, because he was an outspoken lawyer who was not afraid to stand up for ordinary people.

After 1989, the country began its gradual move toward democracy, and in 1997, when the country was preparing for new elections to the House of Representatives, the Ministry of the Interior solicited bids for creating the country's first national identification card. The task was to create more than two million ID cards using all the necessary information about every citizen, which was collected from civil registry offices at eighty sites across the country and stored on a VAX mainframe computer.

At Eastnets, we knew a little about issuing cards. We were producing the Visa cards offered by Arab Bank. A venerable institution, headquartered in Amman, it was founded in 1930 as the first private sector financial institution in the Arab world, and it was ranked in the top one hundred banks in the world. We were already providing it with voicemail services: in other words, customers could phone the bank and get an automated message on, for example, the balance of their bank account. As a result, when they decided to repatriate the production of their credit cards, then being manufactured in the UK, they turned to us for help. Quickly, we swung into action, working with Logika, an Italian card-printing company based near Milan. We acquired one of their printers and handled the entire production of the bank's Visa cards: pulling together the necessary financial information for every customer, creating the card's magnetic strip, embossing the card with all the relevant account numbers, protecting it with the right level of security, and developing all the associated software.

But if we knew a little about issuing cards, we knew a lot about networks and connectivity. On the face of it, phone banking, Visa card issuance, SWIFT payments and national ID cards sound like wildly disparate businesses. But in fact, there is a connection, and the connection is...connectivity. They all involve retrieving information from a storehouse (either a computerized one, as in the case of the banks, or a paper-based one, as in the case of the Jordanian government's civil registry offices) and converting the information into digital formats that can be reproduced as voice messages or readable credit or ID cards.

So, given this, we decided to bid for the Jordanian government's national ID contract.

I'm glad we did.

Putting together the bid was a race against time. I remember we worked through the night. We did not want to let slip this opportunity, albeit one where we were rank outsiders. One of our big challenges was sourcing a card printer. Logika, which we had used for Arab Bank's Visa card, was a financial specialist. For the ID project, we needed a specialist that could mass-produce social security cards. Of course, in those days, it was not possible to google potential companies. It was another year before the Stanford PhD students Larry Page and Sergey Brin launched their search company. But thanks to my sister Rima, who had dial-up access to the internet because of her work in the press office of Jordan's royal court, we did manage to search the World Wide Web using Netscape. Also, we used more conventional tools—subscription magazines such as *Byte* (an influential but now defunct American microcomputer journal), all the corporate brochures we collected from industry gatherings such as the CeBIT conference in Hanover, and most important of all, the insights we learned from our clients, the banks.

I cannot overstate the importance of listening to your clients, your customers. Even though information is now more freely available than ever before, you can be sure that the most valuable information is picked up in conversations with your clients. We heard about the Jordanian government's national ID project through a tip-off from one of our banking clients, and it was another banking client that pointed us in the direction of Fargo.

Now Fargo had nothing to do with the celebrated Oscar-nominated movie by Joel and Ethan Coen that came out the previous year and was set in the US Midwest state of North Dakota. No, this Fargo was a little-known card printing company based in the neighboring state of Minnesota—although it would go on to be recognized by *Fortune* magazine as one of America's fastest-growing companies a few years later.[20] We called the sales manager, and he agreed to supply us with a card printer, if we were selected for an interview. I suppose he thought he had nothing to lose.

After we submitted our bid, we waited and waited. Eventually, we were called for an interview, and we went with some trepidation. Who were we to be bidding against the likes of 3M, the US-based multinational conglomerate, and other big firms from the United States, Europe and elsewhere in the Middle East?

The interview was held in two stages. First, there was the technical, or proof of concept, stage. Could we make an ID card? Yes, we could. But the government was not just going to take our word for it. They wanted us to show them that we could.

So we lugged along with us one of Fargo's printers, with money I borrowed from my brother Ammar, who was one of Eastnets' shareholders. Then we began the demonstration, watched by a panel of experts. It was a nerve-racking moment. All eyes were on the printer. I remember thinking it was taking a bit longer than usual. As time ticked by, I began to fear the worst. Would it work in front of all these people? Suddenly, there was a whirring sound, and the printer delivered our prototype ID card.

That was a magical feeling. We had passed the first stage of the interview. Indeed, we passed with flying colors. As we later found out, ours was the best technical bid. All the time we had spent working on phone banking, credit card issuance and SWIFT banking was starting to pay off. It meant that we could go forward to the second crucial stage of the interview: the financial bid.

Fahed, as commercial manager, had prepared the numbers. He calculated that we could undertake the work for $3.5 million. It was the biggest contract we had ever pitched for, and while we dared to hope, we were sanguine about our chances of closing the deal.

It took a while for the government to make its final decision, but when they did, we were overjoyed. Against the odds, we had won the contract. It turned out that our bid, though large for us, was $1 million dollars less than the next rival bid.

In the end, it was no contest.

But if I had every reason to celebrate, I had to keep the champagne on ice because I first had to find a bank that was willing to provide me with the necessary loan facilities. Since the Jordanian government's payment would only be made on completion of the contract—when we had produced two million ID cards—I needed a bank loan to pay for the printers from Fargo, the blank cards from the Italian company Pikappa, and the services of many engineers. Ordinarily, a bank would have jumped at the chance of making a loan to a government contractor—it had prestige value. But my finances were in such a parlous state that I struggled to find a bank willing to loan me any funds. I may have been working closely with large numbers of banks—providing them with phone banking and SWIFT services. But when it came to loans, they were deeply reluctant to throw what they saw as good money after bad.

Objectively, you can see their point. It was seven years since the first Gulf War, and my original debt of $1.5 million had, because of increasing interest rates and repeated rescheduling, risen to $2 million. Yes, the bankers could see that I was developing a viable business, but they wanted some tangible assets as collateral, and I just didn't have any.

It dawned on me that I may not actually be able to deliver on the hard-won government contract.

I badly needed a break.

It came in the shape of an angel investor, an old mentor of mine: an Arab-American named Khaled Kamal. He was a great supporter, someone who believed in me when others didn't, someone who was always ready with wise words of wisdom. He agreed to speak to the banks and serve as my guarantor. Finally, one bank agreed to loan me the money.

It meant that we could begin the work of creating Jordan's first national ID cards.

* * *

As soon as I got the news that the bank would loan me the funds, I put a call into an office in Minneapolis, the capital of the midwestern US state of Minnesota. I wasn't sure if anyone would pick up the phone because it was just after Christmas, and most people were still on holiday. But after a few rings, I heard a click and the familiar hello of Fargo's sales manager.

We had spoken before when I was looking for a supplier of card printers. Now, after Fargo's printer had performed so magnificently in the demonstration, I was phoning to tell him the good news—and place a $1.5 million order for a large number of printers.

"We won the contract," I said, "and we would like Fargo to provide us with the printers and all the accessories for two million ID cards."

"I don't believe it," he said, the shock in his voice so clear, despite the crackly line.

It was only when I insisted it was true and began talking practicalities that he started to digest the news—he had just been given the most enormous, if belated, Christmas present.

I, however, couldn't celebrate. Not yet anyway. I had work to do. For me, payday would be when I had fulfilled the terms of the contract.

To oversee the implementation of the project, I appointed Majed Abu Zir, one of my most loyal lieutenants. Indeed, he is Eastnets' longest serving employee—apart from me. He joined in 1985, having completed an engineering degree at Jordan's highly respected polytechnic and two years of national service in the Jordanian army. Indeed, I think there was a crossover of about a week when he joined us as he was finishing his military duties. For a few hours every day, he would enter our offices wearing full battle fatigues, having already done a day's work as a soldier.

For the next five months, Majed and his team of engineers moved heaven and earth to complete the project. By May, they had installed card issuance stations in eighty locations across Jordan. These were the hubs where all the information from the country's eighty civil registry offices were to be collected and where the cards were to be printed for distribution to every single eligible voter in Jordan. The final task was to let the Jordanian government carry out its own verification process—known as a UAT, or user acceptance test. The purpose was for the government to establish, to its own satisfaction, that the requirements of the contract had been met.

We were confident that they had—and, soon enough, the government confirmed that it was happy with our work.

The next day, or perhaps the day after that, I received a check for the contract. Immediately, I went along to pay it into the bank. This was one transaction I wanted to do in person.

When I arrived, I handed over the check to the bank manager who had been handling my loan. I could see his flickering computer screen displayed all my financial details. The figure in the debit column was minus two million dollars. Then, with a click of the computer button, that number became zero.

The bank teller smiled at me. And I smiled back. And when I walked out of the bank, I was walking on air. I felt like I was the richest person in the world.

It had taken me seven years. But I was finally debt free.

I was free, at last.

* * *

Even after all these years, I remember that day so well. It was May 15, 1998, and I had reason for a double celebration: it was my forty-third birthday. You cannot measure the tears I shed on that day. They were tears of joy, relief and happiness. They were an outpouring of the anxiety that I had kept bottled up for far too long.

I am a firm believer that you make your own luck. There is no substitute for working hard, staying alive to new possibilities, scouring the horizon for potential opportunities. If we hadn't picked up news about the Jordanian government's RFP through our banking contacts, if we hadn't found dial-up connectivity to the internet, if we hadn't reached out to Fargo, if we hadn't worked through the night to get the technical and financial bid "just right," we wouldn't have got the contract. Even so, I thanked my lucky stars that day. And I thanked the people closest to me: my team of brilliant engineers, my angel investor and my family.

There is a cold, dark loneliness about being bankrupt. I was not, of course, the only businessman to fall badly into debt after the first Gulf War. There were thousands of us. For some, this made things easier, more bearable. I, however, didn't feel that way. When I was bankrupt, I felt it personally. I felt I had failed myself. Worse still, I felt I had failed my family. When I suffered, they suffered too. I dragged everyone down.

In those darkest of times, I took inspiration from a Qur'anic verse that was framed on the office wall of one of my colleagues. It has an oft-repeated phrase: "With every difficulty there is relief." These words helped me see that you should always interpret every setback as temporary, as something that can be turned into something good.

Also, during that time, I came to understand this essential fact of being an entrepreneur: you cannot do it alone. You need allies, supporters, a network of people around you. Throughout those long years, Hanin, my wife, was incredibly supportive, incredibly patient, incredibly stoic. She understood that you can't be an entrepreneur from nine to five. If you're not all-in, then you just won't succeed. It's not a job—it's a *life*. But that has implications for those around you—especially when things go wrong. Sometimes, she and I simply could not afford to go to a restaurant. Other times, we were excluded from social gatherings.

Of course, this made the taste of success when it finally came all the sweeter.

* * *

When you're down, if not quite out, you get used to having doors slammed in your face. But now, as the trusted provider of national ID cards to the Jordanian government, I found that doors started to open, almost magically so.

About a year after the successful launch of the ID cards, I received a call from SWIFT, the company whose services I was offering banks via personal computers. After seeing what Cerberus Software had done with NovaSwift, they had developed their own connectivity solution for personal computers, and they wanted to break into the Middle East market by establishing a hub in Dubai. Today, it might seem obvious why they would want to establish a regional business in Dubai. Back then, however, the reasoning was not so obvious. Dubai was not yet the modern city of tall, glinting towers. The construction of the iconic Palm Jumeirah, a man-made archipelago of luxury villas and hotels, and the Burj Khalifa, the world's tallest tower, were some years away. But those in the know could see that changes were afoot. Sheikh Mohammed bin Rashid Al Maktoum, the Crown Prince of Dubai, made no secret of his ambition to create a kind of Middle Eastern Hong Kong or Singapore. And his chance came when the UK handed Hong Kong back to China in 1997, leaving the future of its former colony as a global financial center in doubt. Sheikh Mohammed lost no time in wisely positioning Dubai as a viable alternative.

SWIFT's top executives could see this transformation, and they called me to see if I could help. Of course, I said yes. In business, you rarely say no. You say yes and then scramble to make good that promise. A deal with SWIFT was the potential deal of my life, even trumping the national ID card project. I could not let it slip by. Also, I knew I was in a strong bargaining position: as a global organization, SWIFT was never going to want to build a hub from scratch—it would have been too costly and, given its lack of local knowledge, too risky.

There was a problem, however. I was based in Amman, not Dubai. Specifically, I did not have an office in Dubai. Fortunately, I knew someone who did, someone I was in talks with about a possible joint venture. He agreed to let me have the office for my crunch meeting with SWIFT's executives. Naughtily, perhaps, I decided that I would not reveal that the office wasn't mine if they didn't ask me. What I would have said if they had asked me, I do not know. But I had to take the risk if I wanted to win the contract. I was lucky that they never asked me the question. They never put me on the spot.

In fact, the meeting went very well, and after further negotiations, I won the SWIFT deal to serve as the company's regional business partner. At a stroke, I was given a client base of 450 banks across the Middle East and Turkey. Not only that, but SWIFT agreed to train my engineers, software developers and sales staff and help me manage expansion in the region.

As the 1990s came to an end, I took the opportunity to look back on an extraordinarily turbulent period. For most of the time, I had been fighting to stay afloat after the devastating impact of the first Gulf War.

But I was ending the decade on a high. Indeed, I was ending the *millennium* on a high.

I had every reason to think that I was through the worst.

"Life isn't about finding yourself," wrote George Bernard Shaw, in words I often quote. "Life is about creating yourself." I had every reason to think that, after weathering all the storms, I was creating a new, and better, version of myself.

Chapter 7

INSEAD, BLUE OCEANS & ACCELERATED GROWTH

ALL AROUND THE WORLD, THE NEW MILLENNIUM WAS welcomed with extraordinary firework displays. There was great optimism, and stock markets surged to record highs. In the United States, the Nasdaq index of technology companies peaked on March 10, 2000, at 5,048, having risen fivefold since 1995.

Then, without warning, the world went into a vicious tail-spin. First, the so-called dot-com bubble burst, and trillions of dollars were wiped off the stock markets. For the previous five years, this bubble had grown ever bigger, pumped up by what became known as "irrational exuberance." Investors, anxious not to miss out on a once-in-a-generation opportunity to make a fortune, shoveled money into the pockets of any company with a ".com" after its name. When they encountered skeptics, when they were accused of ignoring traditional fundamentals, they hit back. Talk of "a new paradigm" was all too common. And for a while, so-called growth investors looked smart.

Many dot-com companies defied the normal logic of investment, seeing their stock price rocket even though they had not
yet generated a single dollar of revenue or profit, nor launched
an actual product or service.

As the market reached its peak, there was suddenly a spate of
panic selling among investors after several of the leading high-
tech companies, notably Dell and Cisco, placed huge sell orders
on their stocks. Dot-com companies whose IPOs had attracted
massive investment lost all of their value in a matter of months.
It was only by some miracle that Amazon, founded by Jeff Bezos,
who is, by some estimates, the world's richest man, lived to fight
another day. The dot-com collapse drew comparison with the
Great Wall Street Crash of 1929 and prompted fears of another
Great Depression.

Then, as if things could not get any worse, Osama Bin Laden's
militant Islamist group, Al-Qaeda, unleashed a reign of terror
on Tuesday, September 11, 2001, a day forever remembered
simply as 9/11. Suicide attackers destroyed New York's iconic
Twin Towers, killed about three thousand people, and set in
train a sequence of events that led to the second Gulf War. Just
as his father had done as president in 1990, George W. Bush
sought revenge, swiftly declaring a "war on terror" and trigger-
ing a military campaign against the Taliban, the Islamic extrem-
ists believed to be sheltering Bin Laden in Afghanistan.

In Dubai, where I was now based after the deal with SWIFT,
we all wondered what would happen next. Were we facing
another long economic winter? Would there be a return to
the dark days that followed the first Gulf War? In fact, these

dreadful events did not affect my business in the same damaging way. Indeed, if anything, my business became *more relevant, more necessary* and, consequently, *more valuable.* Above all, this was because investors from the Middle East, anxious to find new places for their money after the dot-com crash and the 9/11 terrorist attacks, looked for opportunities in the region. Money that had been invested in US tech stocks found a new home in businesses across the Middle East. Dubai was a beneficiary of this new investment focus, and the dramatic change to its skyline is testimony to this as investors plowed enormous sums of money into spectacular high-rise buildings, hotel complexes and other real estate. And anyone doing business in Dubai stood to prosper.

My business with SWIFT was the foundation of my newfound prosperity. It meant I had to travel across the region, overseeing the work of my staff to put banks on the SWIFT system. For me, this was exciting. But one day, I noticed that my corporate adviser, a former EY partner, had a worried look on his face. He could see the company's potential, but he questioned if I had the management expertise to take it to the next level. It is typically at this stage that so many startup companies fail to fulfill their promise—and go out of business. This adviser recommended that I take an executive management course at a business school.

At first, I was deeply skeptical. I was forty-six years old and I was a successful businessman. Why did I need to go back to school now? What on earth could professors in their ivory towers teach *me*—a graduate of the real world of corporate life? It did not help that the cost of the one-month Advanced Management Program was an eye-watering $30,000.

But in the end, I let myself be persuaded that it was a good idea.

And it was.

A few weeks later, I found myself walking through the leafy campus of INSEAD, the French business school in Fontaine-bleau, just outside Paris. I thought it then, and I still think it now: this was one of the biggest, and most important, steps in my life.

* * *

It was more than twenty years since I had last sat in a class-room. So the person who turned up for lectures in Paris was very different to the person who labored in a laboratory in Sofia. In those intervening years, I had graduated with a master's degree, worked for two different companies, founded another, traveled the world, lost more than one million dollars and made it all back again, and settled in Dubai. It had been a breathless, roll-er-coaster period, with little time to stop, think, reflect, plan and wonder how I could do things differently.

In a sense, my $30,000 was buying this time: one month without having to think about the day-to-day running of the businesses. But, as I soon discovered, the investment bought me so much more, because I learned so much in my few weeks at Fontaine-bleau. At that time, INSEAD, which styles itself "the business school for the world," was undergoing a dramatic expansion under the leadership of Gabriel Hawawini, an Egyptian-born French professor.[21] From day one, I felt the extraordinary international breadth of the place. We were put into groups, and mine included entrepreneurs and senior executives from Australia, Brazil and the Netherlands.

The Advanced Management Program was designed for C-suite executives, and its intended purpose was—and remains—to open our minds to new ways of thinking, acting and leading.[22] Under the direction of the course leader, José Santos, a Portuguese professor of global management and coauthor of the Harvard book *From Global to Metanational: How Companies Win in the Knowledge Economy*, it certainly delivered on this intended purposed. Even now, I carry with me a couple of the case studies I first encountered there. Strangely enough, they both relate to the lessons that can be learned from defeats suffered by Napoleon at the hands of British sailors and soldiers—Lord Nelson at the Battle of Trafalgar in 1805 and the Duke of Wellington at the Battle of Waterloo in 1815. It is a tribute to the extraordinary professionalism of INSEAD's professors that they draw attention to the best case studies, regardless of what these say about French national heroes.

Interestingly, the case study on Napoleon's final loss at Waterloo, entitled "Napoléon Bonaparte: Victim of an Inferior Strategy?" was prepared under the supervision of two INSEAD professors, whose ideas on business competition have had a big influence on me: W. Chan Kim and Renée Mauborgne. A couple of years after I left INSEAD, they published their acclaimed business book *Blue Ocean Strategy: How To Create Uncontested Market Space and Make the Competition Irrelevant*. This strategy holds that growth-oriented companies should move away from "red oceans," which are known markets distinguished by cutthroat or "bloody" competition (hence the name "red oceans"), and look for "blue oceans" of uncontested market space. I realized that I had done precisely this when I had moved from phone banking, which soon became a crowded market, to national ID cards, where we could never hope to gain market leadership, to electronic payments.

Above all, INSEAD taught me about the developmental phases of a company: first, there's the "entrepreneurial" phase, when individuals establish a startup company; second, there's the "control" phase, when the startup gets bigger, and it is necessary to install critical management tools (such as CRM or customer relationship management systems) which give the founding entrepreneurs a panoptic view of everything that's going on in the company; third, there's the "knowledge" phase, when the ideas and insights and intellectual property that are often buried in paperwork or trapped on an individual employee's computer are captured centrally and shared across the company; and finally, there's the "people" phase, when the company capitalizes on the ingenuity, energy and expertise of all its employees.

In due course, I would learn about, and be influenced by, another articulation of this developmental theme, one devised by Michael D. Watkins, a former professor at Harvard Business School. In his book *The First 90 Days: Proven Strategies for Getting Up to Speed Faster and Smarter*, published the year after I graduated from INSEAD, he talked about STARS—five developmental phases from "Startup" and "Turnaround" to "Accelerated growth," "Realignment" and "Sustaining" success.

I later realized that, on leaving INSEAD, I had embarked on the "accelerated growth" phase.

* * *

In late February 2002, when I got back to Dubai, I was fired up by my experience at business school. Straightaway, I started to put into practice all that I had learned. I began the long process of converting Eastnets from what was essentially an "entre-preneurial" company into a "control" company, installing new management systems that would allow me to keep track of progress across different countries. At the same time, I started looking for ways to build on my partnership with SWIFT.

Through my Eastnets business, I had already forged valuable connections with banks across the Middle East, and in the months before 9/11, I had begun to have exploratory discussions about launching a new venture with a SWIFT subsidiary called Bolero. After I collected my INSEAD certificate, I resumed those conversations. Now, SWIFT's Bolero had—and has—nothing to do with the short, cropped ladies jacket inspired by the Spanish matador's *chaquetilla,* nor Ravel's sensuous composition that accompanied the gold-winning ice dance of Jayne Torvill and Christopher Dean in the Los Angeles Olympics of 1984. No, this Bolero was a much more prosaic affair, standing for the "Bill of Lading Electronic Registry Organization." A bill of lading is the legal document given to the captain of a cargo ship when goods are first loaded at the start of a journey and handed over by the captain to the buyer at the end of a journey to formalize the transfer of ownership and authorize the unloading of the goods at the destination port.

Originating in a European Union-funded initiative to turn this cumbersome, paper-based, cross-border trade process into electronic formats, Bolero started as a London-based joint venture between SWIFT and TT Club—the international transport and logistics industry's leading provider of insurance and related risk management services. Together, they built the essential infrastructure: a core messaging platform and an electronic title registry. This meant that the ownership of goods could be easily exchanged electronically, thereby expediting the whole process of cross-border trade.[23]

I took an interest in this joint venture because I could see that banks in the Middle East, who were party to these bills of lading, were increasingly involved in the global trade. China was fast becoming the world's manufacturing hub, having just been accepted as a member of the World Trade Organization, and growing numbers of giant transporter ships, piled high with multicolored containers, were journeying from Asia to Europe, passing through the narrow Strait of Malacca and then continuing to the Red Sea and the Suez Canal. Meanwhile, vast numbers of oil tankers were passing through the Strait of Hormuz, which separates the Gulf States from Iran, carrying the black gold that was fueling rapid globalization. Indeed, in the ten years from 1995 onward, the volume of trade between the six members of the Gulf Cooperation Council and East Asia grew fourfold. Not surprisingly, the trade link between China and the Middle East would soon be dubbed "the new Silk Road."[24] Once again, the region was becoming a crossroads for international business, and Dubai was right at the heart of these complex networks.

I approached SWIFT about establishing Bolero MENA. They liked the idea. I also approached potential investors, and they too were enthusiastic: Al Mal Group, a Kuwaiti investment group introduced to me by my brother Ammar (who acted as their legal advisor), allocated $3 million for the venture and advanced $1 million of that to get the business off the ground. This startup, which was independent of Eastnets, was my first attempt at looking beyond my main company, diversifying my interests and, in effect, becoming a serial entrepreneur. It formally opened its doors in July 2002, with a chief executive based in offices in Dubai Internet City, the then relatively new technology park located close to the Palm Jumeirah luxury property complex.

One of the first companies to sign up to Bolero MENA's services was CompuMe, a chain of computer stores across Egypt and the Gulf States. The first bank to sign up was the National Bank of Abu Dhabi, which has since merged with First Gulf Bank to create First Abu Dhabi Bank.

Also, in a sign of confidence in the venture, Bolero International agreed to take a 10 percent stake in the business.

* * *

I was excited by the Bolero venture. But I was keen to learn the lessons of the past and keep diversifying. So while I was deep in conversation with Bolero, I was also deep in conversation with another of SWIFT's partners—a technology company based in Luxembourg called SIDE International.

Like Eastnets, SIDE served as a SWIFT partner, reselling SWIFT services to banks in Europe and the United States. Unlike Eastnets, however, it also offered its own proprietary anti-money laundering (AML) software. In the wake of 9/11, there was growing demand for this kind of software among the banks I served in the Middle East because new legislation, specifically the Patriot Act passed in the United States, obliged banks to take extra precautions to prevent black money from being used to finance terrorist activities.

I had met Luc Desbrassine, SIDE's Belgian founder and CEO, at the off-site gatherings SWIFT held at La Hulpe, south of Brussels, and Opio, a pretty village in southeast France. So one day, I called him to see if he wanted Eastnets to help the company break into new markets across the Middle East. I called at just the right time. It turned out that he was, indeed, looking for an opportunity like this. Pretty swiftly, we agreed to work together, and Eastnets began offering SIDE International's proprietary AML software to a variety of banks.

No sooner had I closed the deal with SIDE International than a Turkish investor I had worked with while launching Bolero MENA came to talk to me about developing a SWIFT-related joint venture in Turkey.

This appealed to me for all kinds of reasons.

I had first visited Istanbul with my family in the early 1970s. We drove there from Lebanon, a 900-mile journey by car. I still recall the thrill of seeing the Hagia Sophia, the Blue Mosque, the sultan's Topkapi Palace and the Grand Bazaar, which was more darkly cavernous than any I had seen before.

I again visited Istanbul as a student, when I had taken the train from Bulgaria to cash my father's check into dollars.

Now, some twenty-five years later, I visited Istanbul once again, this time as a business owner. And what drew me back was Turkey's dynamism, its energy, its ambition and, of course, the potential to make money. The country was desperate to become part of the European Union, and its great corporations, including the banks, were busily trying to align their way of doing business with their richer neighbors in Germany, Italy, France and the UK. Accordingly, several of the major banks showed real interest in joining the SWIFT network. But there was a problem. English was not widely spoken, and this hampered our efforts to complete a deal with a Turkish bank.

From this, I concluded that, if Eastnets was going to be able to connect Turkish banks to the SWIFT network, I needed to create a local venture. So with my Turkish partner Mehmet Tombalak, who invested the capital in return for taking a share of the profits from the SWIFT partnership, I created Eastnets Turkey.

I could not, of course, run the business on a day-to-day basis. As a result, on the recommendation of my SWIFT partners, I picked a brilliant young computer scientist, a graduate of Ege Üniversitesi, one of the country's oldest academies, and a single-minded operator who had served in the Turkish army. Erol Kaya is his name.

His leadership transformed Eastnets' fortunes in what was then one of the world's fastest-growing economies. Among his early successes was a deal with Şekerbank, an Istanbul-based Turkish bank that focuses on SMEs and the farming community. It turned to Eastnets for help with managing some two thousand daily SWIFT messages for international trade, fund management and capital market transactions. Erol and his team recommended that Şekerbank use Microsoft's BizTalk Accelerator for SWIFT to support its digital transformation, provide speedy integration, simplify internal processes and avoid repeat data entry. The SWIFT integration project, the first in Turkey, helped the bank create 75 percent of its SWIFT messages automatically (without any manual entry), and this, in turn, helped deliver savings of $100,000 in the space of six months.[25]

* * *

It was while I was on a return trip from Turkey to finalize the arrangements for the joint venture that another opportunity fell into my lap. My journey, which would end very happily, started very badly. As I was preparing to leave my meeting with the Turkish investor, a snowstorm blew up, forcing the Istanbul airport authorities to ground all flights. I nevertheless made my way to the airport, and I was put up in a tiny, rather shabby, hotel with poor internet connection. Unable to contact anyone, I felt completely stranded.

The next day, I woke to a beautiful blue sky, but snow still lay heavily on the ground, and while the sound of airplanes told me that flights out of Istanbul had resumed, they were still intermittent. I made my way back to the airport, but after I failed to get on to a packed flight to Amman, where I had intended to go before traveling on to Dubai, I changed plans and caught the first direct flight to Dubai.

It was then that my luck turned.

I was just settling down for the four-hour flight, when I became aware that the passenger next to me was one of Dubai's most famous men. He did not know me, but I certainly knew him. His name was Ali Bujsaim. Anyone who had watched the recent FIFA World Cup, held in Japan and South Korea, would know him as the United Arab Emirates' (UAE) international football referee. Indeed, he was accorded the rare honor of officiating the opening match—the first Asian to do so—when Senegal, the underdogs, beat France, their former colonial masters and reigning world champions, in a shock win. Refereeing, however, was his recreational activity. His day job was serving as a senior officer in the Dubai Police and as deputy director of immigration.[26]

We got to chatting, as you do. At first, the conversation was polite small talk. But after an hour or so, we started talking about Eastnets. He showed particular interest in the national ID work we had done with the Jordanian government. He then revealed that the Dubai government was about to begin the search for partners to help with the creation of a fast-track automated border entry process. As a result of its booming economy, Dubai was seeing such an influx of people that Dubai International Airport was becoming a bottleneck, leaving business executives and tourists disenchanted with their first experience of the Gulf State. Sheikh Mohammed, Dubai's Crown Prince, was keen to introduce an automated border control, or "egate" system. He had heard good reports of the world's first egate systems—in Singapore and the Netherlands—and he wanted Dubai to become the third country to introduce such a system.

As we arrived in the Dubai airport terminal, Mr. Bujsaim was greeted by a large posse of border guards. Speaking to them, and pointing at me, he said, "He's with me." I followed him as he swept through the crowded terminal, and I could see what he meant: there were long queues of people waiting to show their passport and get through customs.

Before we parted company, Mr. Bujsaim encouraged me to submit a proposal when the government invited submissions from potential partners.

This I did, and I was thrilled when Eastnets did win the contract. With our partner, Zebra Technologies, a US firm that supplies card printers, we created what we called the Bitaqae system. This controlled everything from data entry, enrollment, personalization and issuance, and produced contactless smart cards that enabled passengers to swipe their cards, have a three-second fingerprint scan, and move swiftly through the airport. Initially, we arranged for the installation of three printers at the airport. Eventually, by the end of our contract, we had installed twenty-five printers in a further twelve locations across Dubai, allowing more than 100,000 people swift entry to the Gulf state.[27]

* * *

Toward the end of 2002, I was reflecting on the success of having struck four new deals—Bolero MENA, SIDE International, Eastnets Turkey and Dubai's egate system. I would have been happy to rest there, but in this annus mirabilis, yet another opportunity came my way.

Once again, it was connected to SWIFT.

After nearly four years, Eastnets' partnership with SWIFT was going well. The company seemed happy with our work. We had successfully served as a reseller across the region, connecting SWIFT to banks in some of the unlikeliest of places. A particular highlight was our success in connecting Afghanistan's central bank to the SWIFT network. It all started when I took an unexpected call from SWIFT's CEO, Leo Schrank. I was on a business trip to Bulgaria at the time, arranging for the central bank to be connected to SWIFT. The meeting happened to be in the lovely ski resort of Borovets, high up in the Rila Mountains. The desert-dry landscape of Afghanistan was very far from my thoughts.

Mr. Schrank said, "I want you to go to Afghanistan. We have been asked to put the central bank on SWIFT." It was a tough assignment. The country was a war zone after the US coalition's invasion to oust the Taliban, who were widely thought to be sheltering Osama bin Laden and other Al-Qaeda leaders. By June 2002, when I took the call, there were thousands of US soldiers in and around Kabul, the capital city. They needed safe access to money. That was where we came in.

When I was in Bulgaria, Erol Kaya was there with me. After my call with Mr. Schrank ended, I turned to Erol and said, "I have a job for you." He did not flinch as I described the mission, and within weeks, he was flying to Afghanistan, where he stayed at the US base. Every day, he was taxied to the central bank by a posse of armed guards. He sent me a photo of his taxi: a pickup truck packed with menacing Afghan soldiers bedecked with bullet-filled bandoliers, their rifles slung over their shoulders. Little did I realize when I struck the original deal with SWIFT that Eastnets would be venturing into war-torn territory.

But SWIFT's executives were impressed with the Afghanistan success, and when they were looking to expand further in the Middle East, they turned to us. SWIFT was founded in the early 1970s, but by the early 2000s, it was facing growing competition from other companies offering payment services. To preserve its market dominance, it decided to switch from a telephony network—it was then using something called X25— to an IP (internet protocol) network. The problem was that the IP network was not yet available around the world—and where it was, it was expensive. So SWIFT's solution was to create a series of what it called "service bureaus." These are high-tech hubs that connect with local banks, aggregate the payment messages, and pass them to SWIFT via a single, superfast IP network connection.

SWIFT approached me in late 2002, and we began discussions. But they were not just going to give me the contract. I had to prove that Eastnets could deliver this kind of service. As a result, I looked for willing clients who could support us. With Erol Kaya's help, I found one in Ziraat Bank, Turkey's oldest, founded in 1863. The bank's chief endorsed our service and, in the first week of April 2003, we signed a new agreement with SWIFT.

It came at a momentous time for the region. Two weeks earlier, on March 21, TVs carried extraordinary pictures from Baghdad, Iraq's capital city, its night sky lit up as the US-led coalition wreaked revenge for the 9/11 attacks with a "shock and awe" bombing raid of astonishing power. What became known as the Second Gulf War provided the unsettling backdrop to our work with SWIFT, which was my biggest deal by far.

Why was it such a big deal for Eastnets? For a start, the running of a SWIFT service bureau was a complex managerial task, and I needed to find someone with the managerial talent to deliver the goods. Fortunately, I found what I was looking for in Rama Chakaki, a Syrian American who had studied computer engineering at George Washington and Stanford universities. I appointed her Eastnets' first chief operating officer, and she oversaw the setting up of the SWIFT service bureau. The target was to enroll thirty banks on to the system. Such was the demand for IP network connectivity, and such was the success of Rama and her team, that the service bureau eventually connected with more than three hundred banks.

The other reason why the SWIFT partnership was a big deal was this: it put Eastnets on the radar screen of several investors looking to support the region's fledgling technology industry.

One of these investors would transform my, and my company's, fortunes.

It is the Industrial and Financial Investments Company (IFIC), the investment arm of the Industrial Bank of Kuwait.

* * *

So much about being an entrepreneur is about making connections. During 2002, I built on my SWIFT connection to build the Bolero business and the Turkish joint venture, and it was a chance meeting with Ali Bujsaim on my way back from Turkey that led to the Dubai egate project. Now, at the start of 2004, I attracted my first external investor—IFIC.

This opportunity came through my work with Bolero MENA. One of the investors expressed interest in the work of Eastnets and welcomed my approach when I said that I and my two minority shareholders—Fahed and Libra Consulting and Collection Bureau, my brother Ammar's law firm—were willing to sell a stake in the business.

After several weeks of negotiation, Fahed, Ammar and I agreed to sell a 27 percent stake in Eastnets. It was a significant moment. At last, I had some reward for all the blood, sweat and tears I had expended in building up the business over the previous twenty years. Also, I had valuable support from deeply experienced Kuwaiti investors with the skills to help businesses grow—and the capital to do so.

Much of my next year was spent putting banks on the new SWIFT IP network. Then, in 2005, a new opportunity came for me to branch out in a new direction. By this time, I had dissolved the Bolero MENA business. Although I firmly believe that it was a good idea, I was not able to devote the time and energy that was needed to make it work. I had too many other calls on my time. In a sense, it was an idea before its time. Digitization was still in its infancy, and the sheer effort required to bring all the key stakeholders to the table—merchants, shipping companies, port authorities, regulators, banks—was too much. So in the end, I had to let it go. But without Bolero, I did have some capacity to take on other projects, if they were less onerous.

While I was on a business trip to Cairo, where Eastnets had put several banks on the SWIFT network, I met an Arab-Canadian called Lina Hediah. Like Rama, she was educated in the United States, having studied applied physics at Harvard University. At that time, she was working as a consultant with the Egyptian Ministry of Commerce. I invited her to Dubai, initially with a view to getting her advice on structuring our technological platform. But she was so impressive that I offered her the new post of Chief Technology Officer, and in February 2004, just after IFIC took a stake in the company, she joined Eastnets.

In her first year, she brought in a fantastic new business: data outsourcing. A newly formed UK company, Counterparty Link Ltd (CPL), was looking for a partner in the Middle East to help meet the growing demand for information on legal entities (corporations, governments and investment houses) that was buried in corporate reports, registration documents and other publicly available primary sources.[28] It was a huge undertaking, but we saw this opportunity as an extension of our increasing focus on helping our clients comply with increasingly stringent regulatory requirements.

We selected Cairo as our headquarters for this business. Eventually, we established offices in the Egyptian capital's Smart

Village, a wonderful technology hub, like Dubai's Internet City. But at first, the business was based not in an internet city but in an internet café.

When we signed the contract with CPL, we did not have an office, we did not have any computers, and we did not have any staff to handle its business. And yet the company needed us to start straightaway. As I've said, in business, you never—or only rarely—say no. So, I said yes to CPL's demands. To deliver on this promise, Lina hired another smart cookie, Enas Defrawy, as the general manager of the Cairo-based business. Immediately, Enas showed extraordinary ingenuity. She went to a local internet café and booked out the entire place for three months. Then, she set about hiring staff—mainly women. And within a few weeks, she was masterminding a team of fifty analysts. In time, this team would win one of CPL's own "Oscars"—an AQUA, or Annual Quality Award.[29]

And the Egyptian data outsourcing business made a meaningful contribution to what was a fast-growing company. In 2001, just before I entered INSEAD, Eastnets was generating revenues of $1 million per year. By 2003, as I started negotiating with IFIC, that number had jumped to $6 million. And it doubled again, rising to $12 million per year by 2005.

At that point, I felt that my business was unstoppable.

Chapter 8

TURNING EUROPEAN

BY 2006, MY BUSINESS WAS GOING WELL—BETTER THAN I could have hoped. And soon enough, I was getting inquiries from a company interested not simply in taking a stake in the business but in acquiring the whole company. The company was N.C.H. (Network Computer House) Group, an Italian business based in Bologna that specialized in global payments and other financial software solutions. During the previous two years, Paolo Ottani, the founder, had been on a spending spree, acquiring niche specialist companies to strengthen N.C.H. Group's market-leading position as a provider of software for banks, exchanges and other financial institutions. As a result, he had established a presence in several markets across Europe. But he had not yet broken into the Middle East market, and given all the excitement surrounding Dubai, he was keen to do so. Acquiring Eastnets, with our extensive business across the Middle East and North Africa, would be a very quick way to do this.

Now, I wasn't ready to sell out altogether. On the other hand, I wasn't going to look a gift horse in the mouth. So I sanctioned my sell-side advisor and my executive team to begin discussions with N.C.H. Group. If the price was right, I would consider selling the business. As it turned out, the price was right, and so progress was swift, and before long, it was decided that I should meet with Mr. Ottani. The big question was: Where should we meet? Of course, we could offer Amman, Cairo, Dubai or Istanbul. In the end, we agreed on Istanbul, for no other reason than that Mr. Ottani was going to be flying in his private jet—and that had a maximum flight time of three hours. From Milan, Dubai is six hours away by airplane, and even Amman and Cairo, though they look like a short hop over the Mediterranean from Italy, are a flight of nearly four hours. By contrast, Istanbul is two hours and forty-five minutes, assuming there are no delays.

I was pleased that Istanbul was chosen as the venue for the meeting. I knew we needed to make a good impression, and our presence in Istanbul showed that Eastnets was not just a Middle Eastern company but also a regional company on a fast-track growth trajectory. At the same time, our Turkish business was still in its infancy, so we could not just rely on the grandeur of the location to impress our suitors. For this reason, I called Mehmet Tombalak, my business partner in Istanbul, and said, "We need to put on a show." To his credit, he got to work on putting together a spectacular welcome strategy. He really excelled and surpassed even my high expectations.

On the appointed day, Mr. Ottani flew into Istanbul's airport in his private jet, and there he and his entourage were met by a welcome party of Eastnets Turkey's representatives and whisked through the crowded streets of Istanbul in a fleet of BMWs. I met him for the first time at a beautiful restaurant affording fine views of the Blue Mosque and the Golden Horn, the narrow bay where the Ottomans had amassed their warships having carried them over land under the cover of darkness in 1453, surprising the Byzantine defenders of what was then Constantinople and securing a famous victory that marked the end of the Roman Empire.

The conversation with Mr. Ottani was conducted through translators—he only spoke Italian—but it was clear he enjoyed hearing about Istanbul's history. It was clear, too, that he enjoyed hearing about Eastnets' business, and after the prolonged working lunch, we continued the conversation back at our offices in the heart of the city. Again, Mehmet Tombalak had thought of everything. Our office, part of a larger office block, was fine but a little cramped. So Mehmet arranged for us to have the meeting with Mr. Ottani in the much bigger office of a neighboring business. Not only that, but he commissioned the creation of a large placard embossed with Eastnets' name and logo and placed it prominently on the outside of the office block. To the casual onlooker, it looked like we owned the whole building. The postlunch business meeting went well, and we had reason to be hopeful when we bade Mr. Ottani farewell.

Over the next few weeks, I visited Milan a couple of times to discuss the finer points of the intended acquisition. I really felt that I was about to let go of the business I had founded more than twenty years earlier. But then, the pace of negotiations suddenly slowed, and I soon discovered why. As part of its expansion program, N.C.H. Group had conducted what was, in effect, a reverse takeover of TAS, a publicly listed company.[30] TAS was listed on the Milan stock exchange, and its acquisition led to a change of leadership at the top. Mr. Ottani took a back seat, and Giuseppe Caruso, a former commercial director of IBM Italia, was appointed chief executive.[31]

Mr. Caruso invited me to Milan. As I walked into his office, I could tell that things were not going to go well. Straightaway, Mr. Caruso made it clear that he had a plan of action—and Eastnets was not part of it. Of course, I understood what he had to say: when you begin a new job, you inevitably want to do things your own way—you want to do things differently. But this did not lessen the sense of disappointment I felt as I flew back to Dubai. My team and I had worked hard on the negotiations. We were happy with N.C.H. Group's valuation of Eastnets, and we were happy with the idea of being part of the fast-expanding Italian group.

On the other hand, the whole selling process had been a big distraction. We now needed to get back to the day-to-day business of running the company.

* * *

In October, I flew to Sydney for the annual Sibos conference hosted by SWIFT. I was hopeful that this annual event would lift my flagging spirits. I always enjoyed the gathering: it was a chance to meet old friends, connect with useful contacts, swap industry gossip, and pick up valuable business intelligence. Also, I consoled myself with the fact that there would be other opportunities in the future—and anyway, at least I had my partnership with SWIFT.

But there, I was wrong. Very wrong.

After touching down at Sydney Airport, weary from the four-teen-hour flight from Dubai, I made my way to the conference. I soon found myself in a meeting with SWIFT's senior executives. I assumed that it was going to be a catch-up meeting, like at previous conferences. But no. It may have been warm outside in Sydney's early summer sun, but inside the meeting room with SWIFT, the temperature was ice cold. After serving them faithfully for nearly a decade, this unpleasant reception was not what I was expecting.

Although they did not put it in so many words—I would find this out some weeks later—SWIFT wanted to drop Eastnets as its corporate partner in the Middle East. Why? Certainly not because of any performance issues, since Eastnets had delivered, time and time again. No, the reason was simply that SWIFT, now led by a new group of executives, wanted to capitalize on Dubai's rise as a regional hub.

This news, coming so soon after the news from N.C.H. Group, might have sent me into a deep depression. It was certainly a double whammy that I was not prepared for—and for a fleeting moment, I pictured myself back running a high street computer store, having lost everything I had built over the past few years. But of course, there was no way that I was going to let that happen. So, during a coffee break at the conference, I sought out a quiet place and thought hard about what to do next. Then, almost instinctively, I reached for my mobile and phoned a man I barely knew.

It was the biggest gamble of my life.

I didn't really know Luc Desbrassine, the CEO of SIDE International. He and I had only met each other once or twice since Eastnets had become a reseller of SIDE International's world-beating anti-money laundering software four years earlier. What I did know, however, was that N.C.H. Group had been negotiating with Luc to buy SIDE International and, in all probability, had pulled out of any planned deal.

I pumped Luc's number into my mobile, and after a few beeps, he answered the call. He was a little surprised to hear from me. "Hello Luc," I said, "I'm calling from Sydney. But I thought you should know that I think your deal with the Italian company is off."

I had no idea if this was true or not, but I figured that given N.C.H. Group had withdrawn its offer to buy Eastnets, it had probably backed out of buying Luc's company too. I could tell that I had struck a nerve. Luc's tone suggested that he did not particularly want to prolong the conversation. But this changed when I said, "I have a proposition to make to you."

"What is it?" he said, a little irritably.

"I would like to make an offer for SIDE." There was a silence. I wondered if the connection had dropped. "Hello?" I said.

He then responded, still a little curtly, "Yes. Let's talk."

The next day, we resumed the conversation, and Luc confirmed that my hunch was correct: N.C.H. Group had indeed stopped negotiating a possible deal to buy the Belgian company. Also, he confirmed his interest in selling his company to me. Those words were music to my ears. But frankly, I had no idea if I could actually afford to buy SIDE International. Although my company was bigger than Luc's, we were SIDE's clients, reselling their very valuable software in the Middle East. In other words, we were less profitable.

As we continued the conversation, I could tell that he had a number in his mind—a dollar figure that he would be prepared to accept. After all my years of haggling, I was used to picking up buy and sell signals—it might be a gesture or some other hint from a person's body language, or it might be, as it was in this case, a tone of voice on a phone call. The dollar figure, it transpired, was $15 million.

It was then that I realized if I was going to be able to buy SIDE International, I would need to seek help.

So, soon after the call with Luc, I phoned Dr. Talib Ali, chief executive of the Industrial and Financial Investments Company—the single biggest external shareholder in Eastnets. He was a big supporter of mine, and he listened patiently to what I had to say. Then he suggested that I make my pitch directly to IFIC's investment committee.

Keen to capitalize on this expression of enthusiasm, I cut short my planned five-day trip, flew from Sydney to Kuwait, and presented my proposal to the Kuwaiti investors at a hastily arranged meeting. SIDE International, I said, represented a golden opportunity for Eastnets to become a truly global technology company. Yes, on the face of it, $15 million was a hefty price tag. But what did that buy? It bought access to global markets through 250 customers and dozens of product resellers operating all around the world. It bought a regional headquarters in Europe together with offices in New York. It bought proximity to SWIFT in Belgium, the custodian banks in Luxembourg, and the Financial Action Task Force on money laundering in France. Above all, it bought ownership of valuable intellectual property—namely, SIDE International's anti-money laundering software. As a reseller, I explained to Dr. Ali and his team, Eastnets was a follower and, as such, at the mercy of organizations—in our case SWIFT—that we follow. But with our own intellectual property, we could break free. I didn't, of course, say that SWIFT looked as if it was about to withdraw Eastnets' status as a corporate partner.

IFIC bought the idea and agreed to invest $6 million in the venture. It also introduced me to Kuwait Finance House, one of the Gulf State's leading banks, which agreed to loan Eastnets a further $5 million in a form of bridge finance. With the $1 million that I personally invested, I was able to meet the bulk of Luc's $15 million price, and I immediately entered negotiations with him. These began with a request to have access to SIDE International's key information as part of a rigorous due diligence process. Unfortunately, we never got permission to enter the company's offices—the executives did not want to alert competitors that the company was up for sale. This hampered our efforts. Even so, from what we were able to glean, it was clear that SIDE International, despite its fantastic products, was in some financial trouble: it had racked up debts, it owed taxes and it had negative cash flow.

But if the findings of the due diligence process were troubling, I was determined to go through with the deal. In my view, it is necessary to look at the world as a glass half full—not as a glass half empty. "Yes, SIDE International has problems," I told my advisors, who were worried that I was about to make an expensive mistake, "but look at the bigger picture. At a stroke," I said, "we can turn Eastnets into a global company."

In May 2007, after seven months of negotiation, I went to Luxembourg to finalize the terms of the deal. I signed, and with a squiggle of my pen, spent $12 million. (The remaining $3 million was to follow, depending on the company's performance.) It was the first time that I had bought another company. And suddenly I felt all alone.

A short time afterward, I really was alone, on the platform of the station waiting for a train to take me back to Brussels. Suddenly, I was asking myself, "What have I done?" Just a few months' earlier, I had been in Milan, on the cusp of selling Eastnets to an Italian company. Now, here I was, in Luxembourg, the proud owner of a Belgian company.

Momentarily, I was wracked with doubt. To calm my nerves, I decided I needed to call someone. I needed to share the news. Eventually, I got through to my father. "Congratulations!" he said, on the crackly line to Jordan. "We have a Bill Gates in the family!"

That made me feel better, I can tell you. And since then, I have constantly thanked my lucky stars that I took the gamble to buy SIDE International. Also, I have discovered a remarkable affinity to the Belgian people. I knew, of course, that Jordanian Palestinians are sometimes labeled *Baljikiyyah* (Belgians) by non-Palestinian Jordanians (albeit in a negative way). I have subsequently learned that Godfrey de Bouillon, the first Crusader ruler of Jerusalem in historical Palestine, was possibly born in Baisy-Thy, a little village in the Walloon Brabant province in Belgium.

But back in 2007, as the train trundled to Brussels, it dawned on me that signing on the dotted line was the easy bit. The business of merging two very different companies—one European, one Middle Eastern—was going to be a heck of a challenge.

* * *

When I arrived in Brussels, I made my way to SIDE International's offices. At the time, they were in a rather unprepossessing warehouse near the city's Pepsi-Cola factory. Inside, everything was rundown. I noticed one or two broken chairs. It was hard to believe that SIDE International's brilliant software engineers had pioneered their anti-money laundering software in such a miserable setting.

As I walked through the offices, I was aware of people pointing in my direction and whispering to their colleagues, "Who is that guy?" Before long, they found out when I called a meeting of the staff and introduced myself. I told them that I admired their work and that, together, Eastnets and SIDE International would make a fantastic combination in the world of finance.

My words were well received, or so I thought. But I soon discovered that in the M&A business, the M is so much harder than the A. Everything, it seemed, was contested. For example, after a few months, I moved SIDE International to smart new offices—none of the chairs were broken. "What do you think of the new space?" I asked one employee, in a casually friendly manner.

"It's like working in a hospital," was the gruff reply.

I knew then that I would need help with the integration.

To start with, I turned to a smart consultant from Booz & Co—Svetlana Tikhonov. Young, dynamic and multilingual (she speaks Arabic, Italian, Russian and Ukrainian, as well as English of course), she was able to help me bridge the divide between the Middle East and Europe. She was educated in the United States—with degrees from John Hopkins and George Washington universities—but she had spent some of her time at Booz & Co leading the management consultancy's expansion in Russia and Egypt.

Svetlana's big recommendation was to restructure Eastnets so that it was organized not around profit centers based in specific countries but rather around capabilities that stretched across multiple countries. So, for instance, an executive in Brussels could have oversight of activities in Amman and Dubai. Likewise, an executive in Amman could be responsible for work across Eastnets' different offices in Europe, the Middle East, North Africa and the United States. This certainly helped create a more cohesive organization and accelerated what was otherwise going to be a very slow and painful integration.

As well as Svetlana, I turned to a collection of senior executives who would, in due course, form Eastnets' first board. It took a good year to put this group together, and I started by approaching Jaap Kamp, a former senior banker at ABN Amro and who, as chairman of SWIFT from 2000 to 2006, presided over the institution when Eastnets became one of its corporate partners. His experience, connections and savoir faire would prove invaluable as Eastnets and SIDE International were put together over the first few years of the merger.

Among the other executives that would join Eastnets and give the company real presence in the banking world were Steffen Schubert, former chief executive of the Dubai International Financial Exchange (now the NASDAQ-Dubai), and Ray Mulhern, a former vice president of the Bank of New York.

With sound advice from Svetlana, and the prospect of a highly skilled sounding board led by Jaap Kamp, I believed that I was well prepared for the task of integrating SIDE International. There was just one vital element that was missing: capital. If I was going to make a success of the merger, I resolved that I needed to find some additional investors.

It was not long before I found what I was looking for.

Chapter 9
WHEN THE IFC PICKED UP THE PHONE

As THE NEWS FILTERED OUT THAT I WAS DOING A DEAL TO BUY SIDE International, I started to attract interest from investors. The first was from Kuwait Finance House's venture capital arm, the Arab European Fund—otherwise known as the AREF Investment Group. It was investing far and wide, taking stakes in companies in Malaysia, in Sudan and in Kenya, among other places. So, you might ask, Why would they invest in a company on their doorstep? The answer is that they saw synergies between Eastnets' business and the financial businesses they were supporting in Africa and Asia.

After relatively swift negotiations, AREF bought a 30 percent stake in the company, investing $20 million in shares and capital investment. This was a significant boost for Eastnets. Suddenly, we were now being backed by two major Kuwaiti investment groups: The Industrial and Financial Investment Company (IFIC) and AREF Investment Group. It was also a significant boost for me personally. I felt my gamble on buying SIDE International was being vindicated. My focus on the big picture—rather than on the small numbers—was being endorsed by seasoned investors with deep pockets.

To a large degree, I had gone out looking to woo AREF Investment Group when I learned that Kuwait Finance House, which had already invested $5 million in the SIDE International acquisition, had a venture capital business. But I did not woo my third investor. The call from the International Finance Corporation (IFC), the private sector investment arm of the World Bank, came completely out of the blue. Until then, I had no idea that Eastnets was on their radar screen. But their interest was a potential game-changer for me. I talked of it then, and I still talk of it now, as a "bingo opportunity." Suddenly, the prospect of creating an enterprise that was more than just a single-person entrepreneurial business was very real. It was as if I had hit the jackpot.

The memorable call took place in July 2007, not long after I struck the deal to buy SIDE International. The IFC contacted me via Eastnets' sell-side advisor. I was informed that they wanted to buy a stake and invest $10 million in the business. This was a thrilling moment. With the IFC on my side, I would not only have the funds to properly integrate SIDE International but also the business expertise and support to build for the future. Acting on their approach, I made a couple of trips to Washington, where the IFC is headquartered. There, I met Andi Dervishi, an Albanian and the global head of the IFC's fintech investment group.

The meetings went well. The IFC liked the fact that Eastnets was a technology company in a region noticeably short of tech companies. Also, they liked the fact that the company was a big employer of women—again, something unusual in the Middle East. Our business in Egypt, with 120 staff, was almost entirely comprised of women, and they were impressed that I had a record of appointing women to prominent positions within the company: Rama Chakaki as Chief Operating Officer, Lina Hediah as Chief Technology Officer, Enas Defrawy as the general manager of the Cairo-based business, and Svetlana Tikhonov as external management consultant.

Negotiations continued over the next year, as the IFC conducted their detailed due diligence process, and things looked promising in July 2008, when I gathered my full board for the first meeting at our offices in the Belgian city of Waterloo. I looked around the boardroom table and felt a real sense of achievement that I had managed to assemble a talented group of nonexecutive directors who reflected what Eastnets had become: a global technology company. There was Jaap Kamp, the Dutch banker; Ray Mulhern, the American banker; Steffen Schubert, the former Dubai stock exchange boss from Germany; and three Kuwaiti investors: Mohamed Kaissi, representing Technology World Company; Hussein Ali Nasser, representing IFIC; and Abdallah Al Kulaib, representing AREF Group. Also, to my great delight, there was Andi Dervishi from the IFC.

It was while I was at another SWIFT conference, this time in Vienna, that I received official confirmation that the IFC wanted to proceed with the deal. They sent me the subscription agreement—the formal request to join the board as an investor—together with the commitment to invest $10 million. To say that I was overjoyed would be an understatement. That evening, on September 15, 2008, I went along to the conference dinner, and I raised a toast. I was in a celebratory mood. Unfortunately, almost no one else at the dinner shared my jubilation because they were just digesting the bleak news from the United States: Lehman Brothers had collapsed under the weight of its exposure to the subprime mortgage market, tipping the whole world into the worst global downturn since the 1930s.

Of course, I did not then know all the ramifications of that fateful day. None of us did. Initially, we carried on as normal, and I began planning for the day when the IFC would be officially installed as Eastnets' first shareholder from outside the Middle East. Naturally, I was delighted when the IFC issued a statement that explained their thinking and seemed to make the fairy-tale investment an unquestioned reality.

> The IFC believes in strengthening the payments infrastructure of developing economies to make financial services more accessible to both small businesses and individuals. We found out that Eastnets, with its product offering and business model, was uniquely positioned to provide a leadership in the region it operates, lowering the cost of access to the payment gateways to financial institutions, while giving them the confidence of dealing with some of the most sophisticated AML tools in the industry.[32]

Following this public announcement, I soon began receiving calls from journalists. As I told one media outlet, "I am delighted to announce that we are poised to fortify our position in terms of expanding our portfolio of premium-quality financial solutions and reinforcing our pool of technical and financial experts because of our new alliance with IFC. This is another important milestone that will spur a new era of growth for Eastnets in the region and beyond."[33]

But not long after this, I became aware of an ominous silence from the IFC. It was becoming clear that the IFC was beginning to drag their feet as they watched the evolving financial crisis start to wreak havoc around the world. I contacted them and said, "What's happening? Where's the money?" I was given a perfunctory response.

"Let's wait a little bit," I recall them saying. "Let's wait until the end of the year to see your performance."

This was a hugely deflating, hugely dispiriting moment. Things came to a head in February 2009, when I once again gathered my full board, this time in Dubai. I was pleased that the IFC's representative was able to attend the meeting.

But my pleasure was short-lived.

During a break in the proceedings, the IFC's representative asked to have a side meeting. I consented, and during our conversation, he told me that the IFC wanted to revise the agreement: it wanted to take a bigger stake and invest $5 million instead of $10 million.

I was dumbfounded. "We have an agreement," I said. "You've even announced the deal on your website."

But he was unmoved. It was a take-it-or-leave-it offer.

My instinct was to say no. But before I made a rash response, I consulted my senior colleagues.

It was not going to be easy to turn down the IFC's offer. Without the cushion of the additional finance, we knew that we would be on our own, our journey would be harder, and the hill we would have to climb would seem steeper. As a company, we had factored the new investment into our business plans. We had an outstanding performance-related payment of $3 million for the SIDE International acquisition, and we had provisionally allocated some of the IFC investment for this. Also, we needed the IFC's remaining investment to lubricate what was going to be a tricky merger. On the face of it, Eastnets was a company with global reach—with offices in Belgium, Dubai, Egypt, Jordan, Turkey and the United States and with nearly 700 clients in more than 120 countries. But we were spread very thinly, with a total workforce of about 370 people: 50 employees in Belgium and the United States (because of the SIDE International acquisition), the same number in Dubai and Jordan, and 40 in Turkey. Our biggest office, in Egypt, catered for 130 employees.

As a group of colleagues, we talked for a while. But in the end, we resolved that we had not worked this hard and come this far only to give the company away in a hurriedly agreed bargain. So I went back to the IFC and formally rejected their offer. To this day, I have never regretted that decision. But I have to say that life did not get any easier after that.

* * *

By the end of the year, after all the trials and tribulations, I had every reason to feel a little glum. But I did not feel that way. On the contrary, I felt optimistic. As an entrepreneur, you have to get used to living on the edge. As the old saying goes, "If you can't stand the heat, get out of the kitchen." I took heart from several things. First, I was now the proud owner of some valuable intellectual property. Second, I ran one of the world's largest and best-connected SWIFT service bureaus. Third, I had significantly increased the company's annual revenues: these had surged to $28 million—up from $12 million three years earlier.

There was a fourth big positive: Eastnets would soon receive international plaudits for its work. In other words, it would soon get recognition as a global player in the compliance and payments solutions market. In 2009, Eastnets was ranked forty-first in the Chartis RiskTech 100 list, the most comprehensive and prestigious study of the top technology firms involved in the risk management market. As such, it was the only company from the Arab World to be listed in the report that included IBM, Fiserv, SAS, Logica and Oracle.[34] In the same year, IBS Publishing ranked Eastnets fourth in the list of companies offering the top-selling anti-money laundering solutions in 2008.[35]

As a result, I was once again being approached by potential investors. Indeed, by the end of 2009, more than a dozen investors had registered their interest in Eastnets. I held provisional discussions with a global software company, while an international private equity firm considered buying the shares of one of the external shareholders. Word of these talks eventually reached the ears of journalists, and speculation was rife that

Eastnets would be sold for hundreds of millions of dollars. As one reporter wrote, "The acquisition could be valued up to $450 million (Dh1.6 billion) and may be the next biggest IT deal in the region after the Yahoo-Maktoob deal."[36] Yahoo had acquired Maktoob, an online services company founded in Jordan and renowned as the first Arab-English email provider, for a reported $164 million.[37]

Amid all this fevered talk, I tried to keep my feet on the ground. This was just as well, because none of the talks with investors came to anything. Above all, I focused on the Eastnets-SIDE International integration, having appointed Freddy Nurski, a former SWIFT employee, as general manager of the Belgium-based operation.

At the same time, believe it or not, I began putting together plans for another business that would take Eastnets in exciting new directions—if it came off.

* * *

In September 2009, I flew to Dalian, the beautiful port city of the Liaoning province in China's northeast, to attend the World Economic Forum's Annual Meeting of the New Champions—dubbed the "Summer Davos." The event, founded two years earlier, brought together more than one hundred fast-growing companies—the "new champions"—that came from rapidly developing economies, as well as technology companies such as Eastnets and up-and-coming executives from the WEF's Young Global Leaders program. The theme of the three-day event, "Relaunching Growth," coming so soon after the financial crisis, seemed very apposite. It was a fascinating experience, not least because it drew together more than one thousand leaders from business, government and civil society, representing more than eighty countries.[38]

Time and time again, I have drawn inspiration from my travels across Asia.

I left the meeting full of ideas, but it was at SWIFT's annual Sibos conference in Hong Kong, which I attended on my way back from Dalian, that I hit upon my next business idea. I was chatting away with an old friend, Jamil Iqbal, chief compliance officer at Habib Bank, Pakistan's largest commercial bank, with a network of 1,450 branches and a presence in 24 countries. He was also SWIFT's chairperson in Pakistan, so the conversation soon turned to SWIFT's new service for streamlining bank-to-bank remittance payments.

With the rapid process of globalization, there were an estimated 1.3 billion people living abroad, including some 200 million migrant workers who wanted to send a portion of their salaries back to their family in their home country. Many of these people did not have access to traditional banking facilities. In the jargon, they were the "underbanked." Instead, they turned to little money transfer kiosks. Not surprisingly, banks and other financial institutions saw this as a big commercial opportunity. Individually, the sums of money being sent back by foreign workers were not huge (we later calculated that they were, on average, about two hundred dollars per worker per month). Collectively, however, they were massive: the total annual revenue associated with these cross-border, person-to-person transactions was an astonishing $400 million.[39] The trouble was that SWIFT's existing system was not designed for the payment of small sums. As such, it was expensive and slow. To address this, SWIFT unveiled its new workers remittance service at the Sibos conference in Hong Kong.

Iqbal told me that Habib Bank had many foreign worker customers—Pakistanis working in countries all around the world who wanted to send money back to their families in Lahore, Karachi and elsewhere. By way of illustration, he pointed to the high number of Pakistani taxi drivers working in Spain who would jump at the chance of having a simple, low-cost way of transferring money to their Habib Bank account.

By the end of the conversation, we agreed that we would find a way to collaborate on this new venture. Back in Dubai, I talked to my software engineers, and we quickly developed a mobile payments system that would allow telecommunications companies to connect to banks and other financial institutions via the SWIFT network and enable their foreign worker customers to top up their mobiles through a mobile wallet or prepaid card and send money back home. In due course, I would secure the patent for this new technology with the United States Patent and Trademark Office. To this day, I am very proud of Patent Number 10062108 for "a mobile remittance computer system and method."[40]

As I developed the plans for a mobile remittances business, I contacted another old friend, Mohit Davar. If anyone was going to know if my business idea would fly, it was Mohit. In 2003, he had established Travelex Money Transfer, a subsidiary of the UK-based foreign exchange operator Travelex, which was later sold to Coinstar Inc, a US-based operator of coin-cashing machines. He now served as chairman of the Advisory Committee of the International Association of Money Transfer Networks.

Always wise, always willing to offer advice, he told me, "I think this is a great idea, Hazem." But then he added something else, which I had not thought about. "You do realize that you'll need a banking license to do this?"

I said, "What do you mean?"

He explained, "Although you would be offering a technology service, you would, in effect, be a financial institution too, and so you would need a license from a financial regulator."

This was a bombshell. But Mohit, who was coming to the end of his tenure at Coinstar Money Transfer, agreed to help. He came on board as director of a new UK-registered company, Eastnets Remittances. Over the following few months, I traveled back and forth between Dubai and London, where we sought a banking license from the Financial Services Authority (FSA) for Eastnets Remittances and for a mobile remittances service called en.MoRe.

In 2011, we were awarded a license by the FSA, and we then struck a deal with Qatar Telecom (Qtel) to provide the technology platform for the global rollout of its mobile money services across key markets. To start with, Qtel—now called Ooredoo—opened a payment corridor between Qatar and Pakistan, where Habib

Bank was, thanks to Jamil Iqbal, an enthusiastic participant. In due course, Qtel, serving 2.37 million customers in Qatar and operating across 17 countries in the Middle East, North Africa and Asia, planned to offer the service across its network.

Toward the end of 2011, I was able to unveil the new service at the event where it had all begun: SWIFT's Sibos conference, this time held in Toronto. Indeed, as we entered 2012, there were plans for a Qtel service to connect Qatar's community of 200,000 Nepalese workers via the Himalaya Bank.

Joking aside, it did really feel that my business was climbing to a new peak.

Chapter 10

THE DAY INTERPOL CAME KNOCKING ON MY DOOR

I BEGAN THE NEW YEAR WITH GREAT HOPES. I WAS BUSY PLOT-
TING the future: the old SIDE International business felt like it
was fully merged into the Eastnets business, I was developing
new opportunities with the London-based and FSA-regulated
Eastnets Remittances business, and I was finding new clients
and new markets for our products and services. But then, on
Tuesday, January 17, 2012, my world came to a shuddering halt.
My mother, who had always been there for me, passed away. She
had been ill for some time, but it was nevertheless a shock when
the end finally came.

Throughout her life, she exerted a quietly powerful influence on all her children. If my father was the family's human
dynamo—full of energy, full of chutzpah—my mother was the
gravitational force that pulled the family together. When I had
taken off to Bulgaria after my father had all but dismissed me
as a lost cause, she whispered in my father's ear, "Go—Find
your son!" And he did.

Now she was gone.

But of course, her influence remained and remains to this day. As the saying goes, "Mothers write on the hearts of their children what the rough hands of the world cannot erase."

She had seen me succeed, fail and succeed again. Thankfully, as a merchant's granddaughter, she understood the ups and downs of the entrepreneurial life. If only she had lived a little longer, she would have been able to share with me one of my proudest moments: in February 2012, I and my company were the subject of an INSEAD case study. Little did I think—when I was studying at the business school back in 2002 and reading all the case studies about Napoleon and Nelson and the Duke of Wellington at Waterloo (some of which I still keep among my files today)—that I would become the focus of such an august institution ten years later. But when Stephen Mezias, professor of entrepreneurship and family enterprise at INSEAD's Abu Dhabi campus, and his coauthor Mohamad Fakhreddin, approached me, I didn't hesitate to say yes. The end result, entitled *Eastnets: Opportunity in Every Difficulty*, was very flattering. They noted that Eastnets, by "[making] the transition from being a startup to being a globally ranked firm...is clearly a story of phenomenal success against all odds." They added,

> The story of Eastnets is all the more remarkable because of its origins in the Middle East, a region that is often assailed for lagging behind other parts of the globe in technology-based entrepreneurship. For this reason, the story of the founders and the firm, from its first street level shop in Amman until it made the transition to an established small enterprise, is one worth recounting.[41]

A few weeks later, I received another remarkable stamp of approval when the Middle East edition of *Fortune*, the US business magazine, put me on their cover. The associated feature article was entitled "Hazem Mulhim: World Banks Trust This Man!"[42] The journalist, Bilal Hajjawi, wrote, "His company's survival and his own story often defy logic," and gave a nod to the recently published case study. "INSEAD, the international prestigious French Business Administration Institute, has noticed. The institute teaches his case as highly successful Arab entrepreneurship that survived against all the odds."

I was, as you can imagine, on cloud nine.

But the sense of celebration did not last for long. As I cracked open the champagne, a different set of dark clouds were beginning to gather. It was almost as if my world, without the reassuring presence of my mother, was entering a stormy, unsettling period. Over the next few months, I was battered by one piece of bad news after another.

* * *

Soon after the *Fortune* article was published, I got a call from one of my engineers in Dubai. He was having trouble accessing some valuable software hosted by our service bureau. A year earlier, as part our business expansion, we had started to host mobile services on the SWIFT service bureau in Dubai. The Qatar-based Qtel service for mobile remittances was the first of these. But in parallel, we had struck a deal with IMUM, the main mobile contractor for Abu Dhabi's Department of Transport (DOT). It was worth $7 million. As subcontractor, we hosted the mobile contractor's software that facilitated the payment of car parking fees. When a driver parked their car, they could pay via their mobile phone, receive a digital ticket and know that the DOT's officious traffic wardens would not issue a penalty fine. For a while, it worked well—until I got that call from the engineer. "What's the problem?" I asked. He went to find out, and he soon discovered that the service had been hacked by a rogue ex-employee of another supplier for the DOT project. Eventually, the highly efficient Abu Dhabi police tracked down the culprit and an accomplice—who were given one-year travel bans. But that did not help my situation. IMUM took a dim view of the fact that our systems had been hacked and used it as an excuse to stop paying Eastnets the $7-million fee.

This was a huge blow. And the news only got worse when Barclays, Eastnets' bank, announced plans to close all its local business accounts. In the wake of the financial crisis, the British bank had avoided being bailed out by the UK government by selling a 30 percent stake to Abu Dhabi and Qatari investors for $7.3 billion.[43] But this did not solve its financial problems, and now the bank was taking the first steps that would lead it to dramatically downsizing its operation in the United Arab Emirates. For me, this was particularly bad news because it meant that I had to pay back the loans I had taken out with Barclays.

You might ask why didn't I just go along to another bank and arrange a new business loan? Well, it was not as easy as that. For a start, several other major banks were pulling out of or downsizing their operations in the UAE, including Royal Bank of Scotland, Lloyd's and Standard Chartered.[44] Also, I was not a good credit risk, having lost my lucrative Abu Dhabi contract. Which bank would be willing to give me a loan—and quickly?

So the double whammy of the lost Abu Dhabi contract and the closure of Barclays' business accounts was an unmitigated disaster. I had salaries to pay. I had bills to pay. I had bank loans to pay. They say that "cash is king." But that is not really the case. What is truly important is not cash but *cash flow*. And by the middle of 2012, I didn't have it.

And my financial situation was about to get a whole lot worse.

* * *

Ever since the financial crisis, the IFIC representative on my board, a young man with a big voice, had been a thorn in my side. We did not really see eye to eye. He only ever seemed interested in the balance sheet. In his view, business was all about the P&L. I, by contrast, was primarily interested in the big picture. I could see the enormous potential for Eastnets because banks and other financial institutions were increasingly being forced to submit to ever more onerous regulations. Sadly, I lost the battle to convince him, and by 2011, as the true impact of the financial crisis started to bite, IFIC had told me that they wanted to exit my business and liquidate their assets.

With the benefit of hindsight, I should have let them get on with selling their own shares. But when they struggled to find a buyer, they approached me. At first, I refused. Why should I buy their shares? But then they started nagging me 24/7. I still refused. But in the end, they made me an offer that I could not refuse.

Well, I could have refused—and I now know that I most certainly should have refused. But at the time, it seemed too good to be true. IFIC offered to sell me their shares at the price they bought them when they became my first external investor eight years earlier. It was not rocket science to work out that if I bought them at 2004 prices and sold them at 2011 prices, I could make a tidy profit and solve my urgent cash flow problems.

There was just one catch: I did not have the $6.9 million I needed to buy out the Kuwaiti investors. Hurriedly, I looked around for investors that would provide me with a bridging loan. I turned to a Dubai-based investment bank that had served as my sell-side advisor in the search for potential buyers of the IFIC's stake. When there were no investors to be found, the bank stepped in with an offer of help. It agreed to loan me the money by temporarily buying IFIC's shares and taking a seat on Eastnets' board. But this offer came with two strings attached: first, I had to buy back its shares for $8.9 million after one year; and second, I had to provide it with a personal guarantee in the shape of a post-dated check for the agreed amount.

At the time, these conditions seemed innocuous enough to me. But my lawyer, David Salloum, who had been with Eastnets for nearly ten years and has never been afraid of saying what he really thinks, raised some red flags. He warned me not to agree to these terms. He especially warned me against signing a post-dated check. But in my wisdom, I thought differently. Yes, I knew that the investment bank would not have been willing to lend me the money if I had not been willing to put my name to a personal guarantee. But as I told myself, I'd raised $30 million before. Surely, I could do so again.

I would be taught a painful lesson.

Self-belief is vital for any entrepreneur. Time and time again, you are told no when you believe the answer can be yes. When you push and push back, and find that the answer is, indeed, yes, you feel vindicated. And the next time someone says no, you push again. But sometimes, the answer really is no. If you continue to push back, then you are lost. It is at that moment that self-belief becomes hubris—and that is what happened to me.

In June 2011, as I struck the deal with the investment bank and signed on the dotted line, I did not give the small print of the contract a second thought. This was because I was already deep in negotiations with two enthusiastic strategic investors. So in my mind, there was no doubt that I would be able to raise the necessary finance in one whole year.

The first interested investor was Thomson Reuters, the global news and financial data company. In addition to its famous news operation, Thomson Reuters had one of the two market-leading businesses providing "watch lists" of proscribed individuals, institutions and companies (the other business was Dow Jones). At the time, the top executives at this business, which has since been renamed Refinitiv following investment from the private equity giant Blackstone Group, saw potential synergies with Eastnets' anti-money launder-ing software. We received an initial approach from Thomson Reuters' head office in London, and then we met Basil Moftah, a smart Harvard-educated executive based in Dubai. Initially, the conversation focused on the potential for a full acquisition but gradually evolved and focused on Thomson Reuters' interest in cherry-picking Eastnets' anti-money laundering and other compliance capabilities.

The second investor was Abraaj Capital. Founded by Pakistani businessman Arif Naqvi, and based in Dubai, Abraaj Capital has since closed, after facing accusations that funds provided by major institutional investors, including the Bill & Melinda Gates Foundation, were misused for private purposes. But at the time, it was the largest buyout fund in the Middle East, and it was especially interested in Eastnets' mobile remittances business. At first, we dealt with Matteo Stefanel, the firm's senior partner in the region. But eventually, we were connected with the top executives at one of Abraaj Capital's investments: Network International, the Dubai-based payments company now listed on the London Stock Exchange. They saw potential for synergies between Network International and Eastnets.

In the end, all the promising discussions led nowhere, and by November 2012, I had run out of time to find a buyer: the year was up, and so too was a five-month extension to the deadline. I had to tell the chief executive of the investment bank that had temporarily acquired IFIC's stake that I could not afford to buy back the shares and pay the $2-million surcharge. Quite reasonably, I thought, I asked him for a further extension. After all, I was able to show that I was attracting investors, and I sincerely believed that it would be only a matter of time before I received an acceptable offer. But the CEO refused to give me more time.

I was, to put it mildly, exasperated.

As a way forward, I asked my good friend, Mohit Davar, who was running the Eastnets Remittances business and who sat on Eastnets' board with the investment bank's CEO, if he would be a mediator. He kindly agreed, and the two men had a meeting. But this softly spoken British Indian was shocked by what the CEO had to say. As I recall, he reported that the CEO said, "We have a personal guarantee, and if he doesn't pay, we're going to go after him. We'll sell his house, his cars and even his furniture so that we can get our money back."

I hesitate to say this, but it was eerily reminiscent of the scene in the *Merchant of Venice* where Shylock demands his "pound of flesh" from Antonio, the merchant who can't repay his loan. It was an outcome I really wasn't expecting. Backed into a corner, I took advice from my lawyers. They told me to do one thing: leave Dubai immediately. That was because under Dubai law, people who renege on a personal guarantee are subject to imprisonment. This time, I did not dare disagree with David Salloum. He had been right about the personal guarantee—and I had been wrong. So, in November 2012, I packed my bags, said farewell to my family, and took the first possible flight to Amman.

And sure enough, within a few weeks of leaving Dubai, the investment bank presented my guarantee check to a bank, and it duly bounced. Soon afterward, a Dubai court handed down its judgment: I was sentenced, *in absentia,* to three years in jail. At first, this did not really affect my life. For a year or so, I was able to travel freely between my offices in Jordan, Belgium, Cairo and elsewhere. I also traveled as part of King Abdullah's official delegation to events in Ankara, the Turkish capital, and Washington. But things changed one sunny morning in the winter of 2013. As usual, I arrived at six o'clock in the morning for my regular flight to Belgium. But this time when I handed my passport to the border force officer, I watched as his face creased in a look of puzzlement.

I said, "Is there anything wrong?"

He replied, with a stern, but not unfriendly, voice, "You have to come with me."

Moments later, I was being escorted to a police interview room. "What's all this about?" I asked.

The officer said, "Your name has been put on a global alert. Interpol have requested that you must be detained and deported to Dubai because there is a criminal request against you."

Interpol is the international criminal police organization. I was shocked. My disagreement with the investment bank concerned a bridge financing arrangement—and it was, therefore, a commercial matter, not a criminal matter. To think that I was now on one of Interpol's wanted lists beggared belief. But either way, it was my personal nadir. Bankruptcy was bad. But this was really, really bad.

I was taken to see a judge, who provided an instant review of my case. He explained that I was lucky: there was no extradition treaty between Jordan and Dubai for what he considered to be a commercial case—so I could not be sent back to Dubai to face the certain prospect of three years in jail. At the same time, as he ordered the police officer from Interpol to return my passport to me, he looked me in the eye and warned me not to leave Jordan just in case other countries took a different view.

It meant that I would be stuck in Jordan until I sorted out my differences with the Dubai-based investment bank.

As I digested the news, all kinds of questions rushed around my mind, making it hard to think straight. Would my clients rush for the door? Would my employees leave the company? Would my friends disown me? Would I ever recover my good name? Would I ever recover—full stop?

Well, I am sitting here today, writing this in my office in Dubai. So you can guess the answer. But, as I will recount in the next chapter, it was a painful time, and it is painful to recall even after all these years. It is all the more painful because I had no one else to blame but myself. I had ignored the wise warnings of my lawyer. I had convinced myself that investors would be lining up to buy my shares and pay a premium for them. In a word, I had miscalculated.

It meant that if I was going to stage a comeback, if I was going to learn from this devastating experience, I had to take a long, hard look in the mirror. I had to look inward. I had to take time for deep reflection.

This is what I did.

Chapter 11
THE REALIGNMENT YEARS

THE NEWS THAT I WOULD NOT BE ABLE TO TRAVEL BACK TO Dubai hit me hard. At first, I worried about the future of my business. It soon dawned on me, however, that I would not be able to see my family: my wife and three beautiful daughters. I was lucky that I had managed to attend the graduation ceremonies of Joud and Masa, my two eldest daughters, who had completed their studies in London while I was still able to travel from Amman. But I realized that I would miss the school graduation in Dubai of Nour, my youngest daughter—one of those milestones that every proud father wants to go to. This cut me to the quick. If this is what the Dubai-based bridge financiers meant when they said they would, in the words of my friend Mohit Davar, "go after" me, then they were successful.

But I was determined to have the last word.

And in my long fight to clear my name, I was lucky to have the advice of my father. Indeed, as I contemplated my future, my one ray of sunshine was the fact that I would be able to see more of him. After my dash to Amman, I went to live with him. It was just the two of us (now that my mother had passed away), and I was able to draw on his immense wealth of experience, knowledge and wisdom.

I, for sure, needed it. I had, of course, faced many big challenges in my life: when I stared into the abyss as I sat on the edge of my student bed in Bulgaria, when my partners set up a rival computer showroom business after striking a private deal as IBM's approved vendor in Jordan, when the first Gulf War all but obliterated my business and left me contemplating emigration to Canada, and when I faced the double whammy of the Italian payments company N.C.H. Group pulling out of a planned acquisition of Eastnets and SWIFT pulling out of our ten-year partnership. On each occasion, I had found a solution, a way out of a difficult situation—a way forward. But now, in the closing weeks of 2013, my predicament was far worse than any I had previously encountered in my life.

As I looked for inspiration, I picked up an old copy of a book I had read after my time at INSEAD: Michael Watkin's *The First 90 Days: Proven Strategies for Getting Up to Speed Faster and Smarter*. I had first read this book in the mid-2000s, soon after its publication and when Eastnets was going through what Professor Watkins (formerly at Harvard and now at IMD Business School in Switzerland) calls a company's "accelerated growth" phase. As I reread the book, I realized that I seemed to be following, in an almost uncanny textbook way, the corporate developmental model he calls STARS which I referenced in Chapter 7, "INSEAD, Blue Oceans & Accelerated Growth."

After the "accelerated growth" phase (the "A" in STARS) comes the "realignment" phase (the "R" in STARS). According to Professor Watkins, successful companies "drift toward trouble" at some point in their evolution.[45] This, he says, might be caused by "internal complacency, the erosion of key capabilities, or external challenges." In my case, of course, it was triggered, as I now freely admit, by my own miscalculations, and then external events came along to compound my problems.

How can you solve them?

There is no question that the realignment phase is serious for any company. As Professor Watkins noted, realignment is "a painful process," and "if efforts to turn around the business fail, the result often is shutdown or divestiture." But he also offered some comforting words. Usually, companies in the realignment phase have "islands of significant strength": good products, strong customer relationships, sound processes or talented people.

Given this, the task of leaders in this phase is "to cut [the business] down to a defensible core and then build it back up."

That is what I resolved to do.

* * *

My first task was to sort out my legal woes—or, at least, begin to do so. In this regard, I was fortunate to have my father by my side. As I have previously noted, he was a British-trained lawyer who was, as the English say, "called to the bar" (not a pub but the collective noun for barristers and their right to practice their profession in a law court) by Gray's Inn, one of the world's most distinguished law societies. But my top legal adviser was David Salloum, who has provided faultless service since he joined Eastnets as our in-house counsel in 2003.

The most important case on his to-do list was the one with the Dubai-based investment bank, which was pursuing me through the Dubai courts. It had successfully secured a verdict against me in the junior court. Now, the case moved to a higher court. If I lost there, then I would be in even deeper trouble than I already was. David's recommendation, therefore, was that I fight back. Accordingly, I countersued on the grounds that my disagreement with the bank was a commercial—not a criminal— matter (and hence a custodial sentence, and the consequent travel ban, were inappropriate) and the one-year time limit was not enforceable by law.

While doing this, I had to contend with a variety of other lawsuits. As a result of Eastnets' financial difficulties—specif- ically, the cash flow problems caused by Barclays' withdrawal from the UAE and the refusal of Iris Modern Urban Manage- ment (IMUM), the Abu Dhabi transport company, to pay East- nets under the terms of our contract—I ordered the downsizing of our Dubai office. Over the years, it had become Eastnets' headquarters, with 150 staff. I needed to cut that number to 50—making some people redundant and moving other people to Amman. Of course, there were many people who were unhappy with this decision, and I faced a legal case, coordi- nated by the workers' union. Some employees, who left or who were made redundant, were happy with my proposal to pay their outstanding salaries in installments. Others, however, resented this, and demanded to be paid in one lump sum. When I refused to do this, they took me to court. In the end, I settled the cases, and the ex-employees were paid in installments. They could have saved us all a lot of aggravation if they had followed the example of their colleagues and accepted my perfectly reasonable offer of payment in installments in the first place.

By resolving this issue, I was able to manage my cash flow problems. Not every legal case was quite so swift, however. I sued IMUM, demanding payment of the outstanding sum due to Eastnets, which amounted to several million dollars. Unfortunately, it was a slow-moving case, and while the courts ruled in our favor, they did not do so until 2017, five years after the company had abruptly, and as it turned out illegally, terminated our contract. But none of this diminished my belief that the legal process was a way to clear my name, clear my debts and clear the decks for a new start. During this time, I also initiated lawsuits in Turkey and Egypt, where my business faced existential crises.

In 2014, I discovered that my business partner in Turkey had struck a deal with SWIFT to be their business partner in Istanbul. This, clearly, went against our agreement, and I sued. It was a challenging case, not least because everything had to be translated into and from Turkish—and of course the Turkish courts naturally sided with Turkish business interests. I did win some compensation, which eased Eastnets' cash flow problems, but I also lost some good engineers, and I was sad to lose a presence in Istanbul, a city I had admired since I was a boy.

No sooner had I sorted out Turkey than I ran into problems in Egypt. In 2015, Counterparty Link, the British company which had contracted us to provide data services, was bought by the Depository Trust & Clearing Corporation (DTCC), a US financial services company based in New York. The new purchasers wanted to close down the Egyptian business—but offered a derisory sum. Had we accepted this, we would not have been able to pay our brilliant employees an appropriate compensation. I teamed up with another of CPL's outsourcing contractors, which was based in Romania, and together we defended our business, refusing to bow to the US company's terms. By comparison to DTCC, we were minnows, but we had some important leverage: it could not proceed with its acquisition of CPL until it had settled terms with us. In the end, we secured a deal that ensured that our employees could be properly remunerated for their work.

* * *

These various legal cases required quite a lot of my attention, but David Salloum took charge of our legal effort, and this gave me the time I needed to carry out a proper realignment of Eastnets' business—focusing on what Professor Watkins calls "the defensible core." Our business in Amman, Belgium, Dubai (where we still had our SWIFT service bureau) and New York revolved around our world-class compliance, risk and anti-money laundering solutions designed to help financial institutions minimize potential risks and losses while adhering to global financial regulations. We had some great products, we had some loyal customers in countries all around the world, and I was fully convinced that we had a great future if I could, as Professor Watkins recommended in his book, reenergize the company.

To do this, I resolved to refresh my top team. I created what I called "the realignment team." There were some familiar faces in this group—including Fahed, whom I had already promoted to chief sales officer, and David Salloum. But I also promoted some other people. One of these was Deya Innab, whom I appointed to the post of acting chief technology officer after Lina Hediah decided to settle in North America. Spending all my time in Amman, I was able to interact with the local staff in a more meaningful way than when I was flying in and out of the place. I came to see that there was a lot of pent-up creative energy and many talented people, and Deya, who had joined the company from KPMG, was one of the most talented. Forward-thinking, fizzing with ideas, energetic and empathetic, she was the embodiment of what I wanted Eastnets to become. It is no surprise to me that she has gone from strength to strength since then, and she is currently serving as Eastnets' chief strategy and product officer.

With this leadership team in place, I was gradually able to reconfigure the business and refocus our efforts on our core competence: compliance, risk-avoidance and anti-money laundering. In my early years as an entrepreneur, I had rejected the advice of many business experts by refusing to diversify. When my business was dangerously exposed by the first Gulf War, I was taught a painful lesson, and when I had the chance to do so, I tried to seize every opportunity to grow the business by diversifying into new businesses and new markets. The years from 2002, when I graduated from INSEAD, to 2012, when I ran into the proverbial brick wall, were my "accelerated growth" years. But on reflection, I probably diversified too much. When I suffered my cash flow crisis, there were just too many moving parts for me to deal with.

Professor Watkins describes how realignments sometimes take place at companies where "the clouds are gathering on the horizon, but the storm has not yet broken—and many people may not even see the clouds." But in my case, the storm had certainly broken, and I simply had no choice but to take swift action.

Fortunately, the steps I took, along with the new leadership team, laid the foundation for the global company as it is today. It was not long before Eastnets became a more dynamic, innovative and fulfilling place to work.

* * *

Every now and then, someone asks me, "How did you cope during those years?" Indeed, even at the time, when I was fighting to clear my name from the Interpol list, I recall my father saying, with a concerned look on his face, "Do you sleep well at night?"

"Yes," I replied. "I sleep very well."

And you would have been hard-pressed to tell that I was carrying a heavy burden in those years. Every day, after taking breakfast with my father, I would go to Eastnets' offices in Sheimsani, near Amman's banking district. As I arrived, I would put on what I call my "happy face," and for the rest of the day, I maintained an upbeat demeanor, making every effort to convey optimism. I did not think that sharing my worries would serve much purpose.

No doubt the anxiety that I felt exacted some kind of toll. But to a significant degree, I was only experiencing one of the periodic downs that entrepreneurs must expect to experience in a life that, by definition, has more than its fair share of ups and downs. And over the years, I have found strategies to deal with the stress that, as they say, comes with the territory. Perhaps the most important is the propensity to "park" a problem. So, for example, I managed to park my legal problems by handing over day-to-day responsibility for them to David Salloum. I would check in with him, but I let them run their course, and ultimately, we resolved the cases to our satisfaction every time.

I think I probably learned this trick from my father. How could he come out of prison with a big beaming smile on his face? Somehow, he managed to stay positive, and I believe he found a way to put his biggest problems to one side—to park them—so that he could focus on moving forward. These days, when I try to explain what I mean, I liken it to the classic problem-solving technique I was taught by one of my math teachers. "If you come across an equation you can't solve," he said, "draw a margin on the page, put it there while you solve the easier problems, and go back to it at the end: you may still find that you can't solve it, but at least you won't have wasted time and missed out on gaining marks on the easier questions."

Parking the problem was one strategy I found useful. Another was physical exercise. At the end of every working day, I would stop by the gym on the way home and pound the treadmill for ninety minutes. That was a marvelous stress-reliever. A third strategy was hiking in the hills above the Jordan Valley. This, I believe, was the most beneficial of all. Every day, I was pretty much tied to my desk, confined within the walls of the office. Metaphorically speaking, I was climbing mountains just to get through all the work I needed to get through. By contrast,

I found the experience of climbing *real* mountains extraordinarily liberating. Reaching the summit, breathing in the clean air, taking in the wide panoramic views—it was wonderful. There is something deeply restful about putting one foot in front of the other and climbing to the very top of a mountain. As you ascend ever higher, you have to watch your step. With stony paths and steeply descending slopes on either side, you really can't afford to think about anything else. I found it a remarkably effective way of banishing all the troubles from my mind.

At first, I went on my own, taking off on a Friday and sometimes staying overnight. Eventually, I invited friends and work colleagues to join me. Sometimes, we would number twenty or more. It was a great bonding experience. I got to know them, and I got to know Jordan better than I ever had before. In the winter, we would head to a couple of places in the north of the country. One of my favorite destinations was—and remains—Ajloun. There, I would visit the twelfth-century fort that sits atop one of the hills and was used by Saladin's generals when defending the region from incursions by the Crusaders. Another was the Roman ruins of Gadara near the modern town of Umm Qais close to Jordan's northern border with Israel and Syria. From the ridge, it is possible to see Lake Tiberias, otherwise known as the Sea of Galilee, and the Golan Heights.

During the summer, we would travel to the south of Jordan. There, we liked to spend time at Wadi Rum, the desert landscape dotted with castle-like rock formations which formed the backdrop of David Lean's Oscar-winning movie *Lawrence of Arabia*. The celebrated British soldier passed through the region several times while helping with the Arab Revolt against Ottoman rule in 1916–1917. Later, he would write about his time there, describing it as "vast, echoing, and God-like."[46]

I would come back from these trips fully recharged—physically and mentally. There was only one time that I really regretted being there. I will never forget the day.

It was June 25, 2015.

* * *

I was out hiking when my mobile phone rang. It was my father. He was calling from Geneva, where he had gone for a short holiday. By then in his late-eighties, he was as active as ever. There seemed to be no stopping him. But on this occasion, he sounded a little tired and a bit anxious, as if he needed my help. He knew that I could not travel, and so, rather bizarrely, he asked me to ask my brother, Ammar, if he could fly to Switzerland and pick him up. As soon as the call ended, I tried to contact Ammar, who was based in Kuwait.

As I later learned, my father dropped dead about an hour after that call. It turned out that he had gone swimming in hotel pool—it was a hot summer that year—and developed pneumonia soon afterward. It was devastating news for me, my brothers and sister. None of us saw it coming. But as I reflected in the months after that day, I was so thankful for the time I spent with him in Amman. Throughout my life, I had my differences with him. Yet, in those final precious years, we had a meaningful *rapprochement*. I must have disappointed him as a boy. By the end, however, he respected me for what I had achieved—and he told me so. "You have made it on your own," he once said. "You have built your business out of nothing, and I am proud of you." I can't tell you how much that meant—and still means—to me. That kind of paternal recognition, after all those years, was like winning an Olympic gold medal.

I was also thankful for one other thing. Just before my father died, he heard the news that I had won my long legal case against the Dubai-based investment bank that had acquired IFIC's stake. "Now," he said, "you can agree to terms and get on with the rest of your life." And that is exactly what I did. Later that year, the new CEO of the investment bank came to Amman, and we settled our disagreement. I bought back some of the shares, and he agreed that the bank would stay on as a primary investor—and it remains an investor to this day.

Finally, in May 2016, I was given permission to travel to Dubai. A few hours later, I was on an airplane, flying back to see my family. Almost four years earlier, I had left in a hurry, promising my wife that I would return in a couple of weeks. Now, I was about to press the reset button and try to get back to normal.

But I was being overoptimistic. As I would soon be reminded, in an entrepreneur's life, there is no such thing as normal.

In my time in Amman, I had changed. How could I not have done so? As the Japanese writer Haruki Murakami once wrote, "When you come out of the storm, you won't be the same person who walked in. That's what this storm's all about."[47]

Chapter 12

EDWARD SNOWDEN, THE NSA & ME

Soon after stepping off the airplane at Dubai International Airport, I rushed home to see my family. I knew that I would never be able to reclaim all those lost years away from them. I knew that I was not going to be able to turn back the clock. All three of my daughters had blossomed into young women: my two eldest, Joud and Masa, had graduated from university; my youngest, Nour, was studying in London. Nevertheless, I resolved to do everything I could to be there for them when they needed me.

It was a joy to be back with my family. But I confess that I did not find the process of settling back into the old routine quite as easy as I thought it was going to be. For a start, at work, there was a different atmosphere to the one I had left behind when I had hurriedly left Dubai four years earlier. Back in 2012, there were 150 people working in the Eastnets offices in the Dubai Internet City (DIC), which served as the company's headquarters. Now, after all the downsizing, there were only forty people, and we were housed in a smaller office in the DIC.

Also, there were things I started to miss about Jordan. I missed the hiking. I missed the day-to-day interaction with my colleagues there. I even missed Amman's small, crowded, noisy streets. Every now and then, I have a debate with my family: "If you had to choose, would you pick Dubai or Jordan?" It is a debate I have never won. My family love Dubai. Of course, my daughters grew up there, so you wouldn't expect them to take a different view. It is young, vibrant, forward-looking, fashionable, there's a party atmosphere, and the architecture is bold, modern and reflects in a very physical way the upward trajectory of the whole place. As you can tell, I too love Dubai. It is, after all, the place where I chose to raise my family and build my company into a global business. But there is something about Jordan that speaks to me in a way no other place does. I have lived in many countries around the world. But Jordan has an earthiness that I like: the bustling streets, the old buildings, the cool summer breezes carried by the fresh westerly winds from the Mediterranean, the proximity to my father's birthplace in Halhul, the friendly people who are never too busy to stop for a chat. Whenever I'm pushed to answer the question "Where's home?" I can't help but answer, "Jordan."

Despite all this, life was good after my return to Dubai. I felt that things were looking up. But I have learned over the years that you can never, as an entrepreneur, sit back and relax. If you do, something is likely to rise up and hit you in the face.

And this is precisely what happened to me on April 14, 2017.

I recall the day vividly. It was a Friday, late in the day, and I glanced at my mobile, which had only been in silent mode for a short while. To my amazement, it showed that I had missed several calls. When I looked at my WhatsApp messages, I was almost paralyzed by what I read. I was being asked to come back to the office *immediately*.

Not long after, I was sitting with my colleagues, watching the news on the TV. We were all blinking incredulously at the screen. Quite unbelievably, Eastnets was one of the top stories. CNN, BBC, CNBC—you name it, they were all reporting that we had been hacked ten years earlier by the NSA—the National Security Agency, the United States' largest intelligence organization and the world's best-funded spy force. As I have said, I sometimes make sense of the world by drawing parallels with great movies. On this occasion, the words "Houston, we have a problem," which were spoken by Tom Hanks in the Hollywood blockbuster *Apollo 13*, popped into my mind.

I called an urgent meeting with my engineers. Not everyone was in the office. Deya and Robbert de Wreis, my Dutch chief technology officer, were traveling in Asia, where they were promoting our new products for combating financial crime. Eventually, we tracked them down in Japan. When we told them the news, Robbert simply did not believe it. By contrast, Deya turned her thoughts to what we should do and prepared a plan of action, which we enacted. Meanwhile, I responded to media requests for an interview with a formal statement: "The reports of an alleged hacker-compromised Eastnets Service Bureau network [are] totally false and unfounded," it began. "The Eastnets Network

Internal Security Unit has run a complete check of its servers and found no hacker compromise or any vulnerabilities." The statement concluded: "The photos shown on Twitter, claiming compromised information, [are] about pages that are outdated and obsolete, generated on a low-level internal server that [has been] retired since 2013."[48] In some additional words that came to haunt me in the days following these revelations, I told *The National*, the preeminent newspaper in the Middle East: "East-nets continues to guarantee the complete safety and security of its customers' data with the highest levels of protection from its SWIFT-certified service bureau."[49]

How wrong I was.

Over the next few days, the true story of what had happened started to leak out.

It all began after 9/11.

* * *

As part of its wider War on Terrorism, the US government wanted to clamp down on terrorist financial networks that were funding extremist groups such as Al Qaeda. Accordingly, it approached SWIFT and struck a secret deal allowing the Central Intelligence Agency (CIA) to receive a blind copy of every financial transaction that passed through the company's systems. Remember, SWIFT carries transactions worth trillions of dollars every single day of the year. At the time, more than eleven million transactions involving around $6 trillion took place on a daily basis.[50] As one US government official noted, SWIFT, then run by New Yorker Leonard Schrank, was "the mother lode, the Rosetta stone" for financial data.[51]

No one knew about the deal—not the banks, not the governments where those banks were headquartered. Only a few of SWIFT's directors were in the know.

The secret US government surveillance program, which was run by the CIA and overseen by the Treasury Department, was said to have played a key role in tracking the financial activities of people suspected of having ties to Al Qaeda, the terrorist organization responsible for the 9/11 attacks. The covert operation carried on until 2006. It might have continued for much longer. But in June that year, the *New York Times* broke the story in a 3,500-word article entitled "Bank Data Is Sifted by U.S. in Secret to Block Terror."[52] The *New York Times* story, based on interviews with nearly twenty former government officials and industry executives, sparked an enormous hue and cry. President George W. Bush attacked the messenger, saying that the newspaper's decision to publish did "great harm to the United States of America" and "[made] it harder to win this war on terror." Some others went further.[53] A Republican Senator from Kentucky called on the US attorney general to investigate the newspaper for treason.[54]

With the details of its eavesdropping exposed in the media, the US government was obliged to try a different tack: it decided to target the small service bureaus used by SWIFT, including ours in Dubai. At the time, SWIFT had seventy-four service bureaus, and for all we know, the NSA targeted many of these in their quest for information about Al Qaeda terrorists.[55] A majority of SWIFT's banks connected to the SWIFT network through these bureaus since they were able to avoid the costs of establishing and maintaining their own SWIFT connectivity infrastructure. But Eastnets Service Bureau was amongst the biggest, and since many of the 9/11 hijackers came from Saudi Arabia and the UAE, it was our service bureau that got all the attention.

To break into our systems, the US government turned to a special hacking unit within the NSA called the Office of Tailored Access Operations—TAO, for short.[56] Over the next few years, TAO's cybersecurity operatives hacked into the SWIFT-Eastnets system—and, of course, with the full power of the US government, they were, indeed, able to do so.

Again, they might have continued to do this, but on that Friday in April 2017, their secretive work was exposed not by the *New York Times* or another media organization but by a group of hackers that went by the name of "Shadow Brokers." The previous year, this group, which was reportedly affiliated with the Russian government, had published reams of secret NSA material online. Specifically, this related to an arsenal of special hacking tools that the NSA operatives had developed— all designed to bypass computer firewalls, exploit vulnerabilities in the Microsoft Windows operating system and penetrate the Linux systems most commonly used on Android phones.

Then, everything went eerily quiet. Until April, when Shadow Brokers revealed how the NSA had hacked into our service bureau. As the *New York Times* reported,

On Friday, just when its leaks had appeared to slow, the group released what appears to be its most damaging leak so far: a trove of highly classified hacking tools used to break into various Microsoft systems, along with what it said was evidence that the N.S.A. had infiltrated the backbone of the Middle East's banking infrastructure.[57]

If there was one consolation, it was that Eastnets was not the only SWIFT service bureau mentioned by Shadow Brokers. The other one was Business Computer Group, one of our partners, which is based in Panama and which serves banks in Latin America. But it was not much of a consolation. At the time, observers said that this was the most damaging of all the data dumps by Shadow Brokers.

It was certainly damaging for Eastnets—and for me. I had built the company as a trusted third party and a specialist in combating financial crime, and here we were, having our own firewalls breached by hackers.

My first instinct was to deny that this was happening—hence my statement. I now know this was hasty and unwise. I should have bided my time, taken expert advice, issued a holding statement until I could verify the facts. But you have to remember that I had no experience of being swept up in a hurricane-force media storm. Not many people do. And I can tell you that it is very hard to think clearly when you are being bombarded by questions from every conceivable direction. Our phones were ringing off the hook. I was asked for my reaction, and I gave it. Also, I was not alone making the statement that I did. SWIFT issued a similar statement at the time: "We have no evidence to suggest that there has ever been any unauthorized access to our network or messaging services."[58]

But it soon became clear that this story was not about Eastnets. We were just the collateral damage, caught in the crossfire of a bitterly fought pseudo war being waged between the United States and Russia. A week earlier, President Donald Trump had sanctioned a US Tomahawk missile attack on the Shayrat airbase in Syria, one of Russia's allies. This was a reaction to the Syrian government's alleged chemical attack on its own people at Khan Shaykhun during the devastating civil war. The Shadow Brokers' revelations, coming so soon after that US attack (and after a long period of silence), were viewed as a Russia-backed calculated attempt to embarrass the United States.

Soon after I made my defensive denial, the world's most famous whistle blower, Edward Snowden, entered the fray. In a telling Tweet, the former NSA contractor, who had first disclosed the extent of the US spying activities before escaping to Russia back in 2013, confirmed that the Shadow Broker documents were genuine. He said the revelations were "the Mother of all Exploits"—a sly reference to a massive 21,600-pound incendiary device, dubbed "the Mother of all Bombs," which had recently been dropped by the US military in Afghanistan.[59]

And indeed, they were genuine.

Using Twitter as its social media platform of choice, Shadow Brokers published PowerPoint documents and Excel files listing computers connected to our service bureau (as well as usernames and passwords) and so-called zero-day exploits—software vulnerabilities that were previously unknown, even to the companies that created the software. According to one report at the time, and as we ourselves later confirmed, one spreadsheet indicated that "a box has been implanted and we are collecting"—code for the fact that covert spyware had been installed on several computers.[60]

In the wake of these revelations, the investigations began. How had the hackers (the NSA) managed to be hacked? Some just could not believe it, and when Shadow Brokers first emerged the previous year, the eye of suspicion had fallen on potential insiders, including a man called Harold T. Martin III who, like Snowden, was a contractor for Booz Allen Hamilton, a management consulting company. He was arrested after computers and electronic devices storing "many terabytes of information" were found in his house, car and even his garden shed.[61] But when the leaks continued, investigators started to conclude that, perhaps, some of the world's best hackers really had, themselves, been hacked.

Before too long, the media caravan moved on. There were other global cybersecurity crises to report on: the UK's National Health Service was hacked, forcing hospitals to turn away patients; thousands of employees at Mondelez International, the maker of Oreo cookies, had their computers completely wiped of all their data; and FedEx, the logistics company, suffered a cyber-attack that cost $300 million after deliveries were stopped.[62] All of these were the direct consequence of the Shadow Brokers' disclosure of the NSA's own cyber tools.

But even if we were no longer in the news, the crisis was not yet over.

The media storm may have blown over, but I was left to pick up the pieces.

* * *

I quickly realized that I needed expert help. So to start with, we hired a specialist cybersecurity consultancy to remove all the malware, install new protections, and generally upgrade the whole network. Also, we hired more software engineers and cybersecurity specialists and worked with SWIFT, which, after all, was responsible for certifying our service bureau and did so on an annual basis.

It was during our own cleanup operation that we finally made sense of something that had taken place, on and off, since 2006. Every now and then, there would be a glitch in the system. Our banking customers would call us to complain that they could not access the SWIFT system. When this happened, we used to call SWIFT to see if they could work out why it was happening. They never could, but they suggested a simple solution: switch off the network and then switch it on again. It was a bit like rebooting your computer, but it worked. What our investigators discovered was that these glitches were caused by the secret spying activities of the NSA's operatives. Eventually, they found themselves stuck in the system, and the only way they could slip away was when we had switched off the system. In those few minutes, they were able to escape the system and escape detection.

But I was not just facing a technology crisis. I was also facing a reputational crisis. Angry clients were, understandably, phoning us, asking questions and demanding answers. "What on earth is going on?" they said. "How could this have happened? Is our money safe? Can we trust you?" If I did not take swift action, I risked a mass walkout of clients.

For help, I turned to Brunswick, one of the world's top PR agencies, which has a presence in Dubai. The man who led their crisis management team was Will Anderson, a former British soldier who had served as a helicopter pilot in Afghanistan and who had been honored with an MBE in the New Year's Honors List. Dynamic, energetic and a smart strategic thinker, he and his team helped us craft our response to clients, the media and investors. All of this came together when we hosted a client conference in Dubai. Many banks came, began to understand our position, and from that point onward, we were able to put the business back on track.

In the end, we did lose some clients who were worried that if it had happened once, it could happen again. But most of our clients remained loyal. They appreciated that no company can ever be entirely safe from governments determined to break into a system and willing to direct their very considerable resources to doing so. Also, they were reassured that there had been no financial losses. The previous year, cyber thieves hacked into SWIFT's systems and managed to steal $81 million from Bangladesh's central bank. So there were legitimate fears among some of our clients that they, too, may have lost money. But no, the NSA took data, not dollars.

In the years since the NSA crisis, I have reflected on what I learned from this episode. They say that what doesn't kill you makes you stronger, and I do think that Eastnets once again proved its resilience. Certainly, we are better prepared than ever. We now have a dedicated security unit that is constantly scanning the system for spyware, ransomware and other types of malware. So if anything like this were to happen again in the future, we have the tools to deal with it.

But I sincerely hope that it does not happen again. It was something to experience once, but not twice.

Chapter 13

LOOKING TO THE FUTURE

When the desert sand started to settle after the media storm whipped up by the NSA hacking story subsided, I was able to turn my attention back to what I had begun when I returned to Dubai after an absence of four years: working out "What's next for Eastnets?"

After a period of realignment, I felt the company was entering what Professor Michael Watkins calls the "sustaining success" phase: the second "S" in his compelling STARS corporate framework. It had shown extraordinary resilience, and I knew I now needed to position it for the challenges ahead. How was I going to do this? I resolved that I needed to take a strategic, operational and individual approach. This has been marvelously articulated by three INSEAD professors: Ian Woodward, Paddy Padmanabhan and Sameer Hasija. In their book *The Phoenix Encounter Method*, cowritten with *New York Times* bestselling author Ram Charan, they write about how "leaders must learn to see their world from three very different perspectives: 50,000 feet, 50 feet and 5 feet. These altitudes correspond, respectively, to strategic, operational, and personal levels of leadership engagement."[63]

To see the world from fifty thousand feet, I started flying around the world. Okay, the airplanes only flew at 36,000 feet, but I was able to enjoy the broader perspective you only get when you get up high. I traveled to Eastnets' ten offices scattered across the Middle East, Europe and the United States; I attended conferences in Cape Town, London, Moscow and New York; and I spoke at several INSEAD events in Abu Dhabi, Fontainebleau and Madrid. All the while, I listened, I picked up tidbits of news, and I scanned the horizon for big trends. It was soon clear to me that the NSA media storm was nothing compared to what the three INSEAD professors call the "firestorm" of change brought about by digitalization.[64] Today, more than half the world's population—some 4.5 billion people—have access to the internet. This means two things: we are more connected than ever before, *and* we must expect more change over the coming years as the rest of the world's population finally gets access to the internet.

Quite what this change will be is hard to predict. If you had told me in 1984, when I launched the Jordan Computer Centre, that I would be running a niche global company that focuses on countering cyberattacks, money laundering, terrorist finance and other fraudulent activities in the banking industry, I wouldn't have believed you. Now, nearly forty years later, it is no easier to predict what will happen next. Indeed, if anything, it is harder, such is the pace of change. But of course, entrepreneurs must continue to prepare for the future. The moment you stop doing this, you're sunk.

We are, I have no doubt, at the start of what some observers are calling "the Fourth Industrial Revolution." The first, which began in the 1700s, saw the invention of machines powered by coal and other fossil fuels. The second, which straddled the end of nineteenth century and beginning of the twentieth century, was driven by electricity, the telegraph, the wireless radio, TV and mass production. The third, which began in the 1950s, witnessed the arrival of computers and digital systems such as the internet which enabled new ways of generating, processing and sharing information. And now the Fourth Industrial Revolution promises to harness the power of machines and the power of humans in new ways.[65] Already, some are referring to "bionic" companies that augment the best qualities of people— their creativity, their common sense, their empathy—with the undoubted qualities of the latest digital technology.[66]

Certainly, as I scanned the horizon from fifty thousand feet, it was the diversity of new digital technologies that made me realize that Eastnets needed to act fast. Artificial intelligence, big data analytics, blockchain, cloud computing, machine learning and robotics—they were all beginning to have a profound impact on business, on society, on everything, in fact.

In their book *Age of Discovery*, Oxford professor Ian Goldin and his coauthor, Chris Kutarna, observe that "what we lack, and so urgently need, is perspective." With perspective, they explain, we can "better assert our own will upon the wider forces rocking the world." From their perspective, the biggest force is, unquestionably, digital technology. Its invention, they argue, represents "a second Gutenberg moment" that is leading to a "Second Renaissance"—in the same way that the German merchant Johannes Gutenberg's printing press sparked the first Renaissance in the 1450s.[67]

Satya Nadella, Microsoft's chief executive, is right when he says that these technologies "foreshadow socioeconomic change ripped from the pages of science fiction."[68] But what does it mean in the financial world—the world where Eastnets operates? I have always thought of the financial industry as a good bet. It was, of course, in the wake of the first Gulf War, after I had returned from Canada, that I first discovered that banks are the great survivors, even during the direst of times. And all these years later, this remains the case. Even in countries blighted by war, such as Libya and Yemen, there are banks managing to survive and that are eager to do the right thing by international regulations.

The advent of digital technology has changed the way people want to bank: typically, they want, and expect, an instant service. To meet their needs, new businesses have emerged to cater for them: so-called challenger banks and a vast number of fintech companies that live in the cloud and have no physical presence on the high street. "Technological innovation has the power to create new services for consumers but also to reshape financial market structures," noted Denis Beau, first deputy governor of the Bank of France, in a widely quoted comment. "The whole value chain is being impacted by fintechs as well as by BigTechs, which are introducing almost every day new ways to pay, to provide credit, to get insurance and, of course, to invest within capital markets."[69]

Meanwhile, the financial industry has become a new arena for the increasingly heated cold war between China and the

West. The Chinese government has made AI one of the central features of its bold "Made in China 2025" plan to transform the country's economy—and it wants to be the global leader in the technology by 2030. This is a significant move. China and the United States appear to be racing each other to be the country that sets the global standard in this technology. Long ago, Werner von Siemens, the nineteenth-century German industrialist and innovator who founded the eponymous company, said: "He who owns the standards, owns the market."[70] More recently, Vladimir Putin, president of Russia, the United States' previous cold war rival, observed, "Whoever becomes the leader in this sphere will become the ruler of the world."[71]

China's banking industry is expected to be a big beneficiary of this technological push. The country is already the world's biggest market for mobile payments: in 2017, the value of mobile payments overtook the combined totals of Visa and Mastercard for the first time. This is expected to increase with the rise of e-yuan, China's "digital renminbi."[72] In a bid to undermine the dominance of China's privately owned fintech giants—Alipay (owned by Ant Financial, an affiliate of e-commerce giant Alibaba) and WeChat Pay (owned by Tencent)—the Chinese government has been handing out so-called red packets containing digital renminbi worth Rmb200 (about $30) that can be downloaded on a mobile phone. For now, this is a domestic currency.[73] But in due course, China may use its digital currency to make international trade settlements, and this may be when it challenges the global supremacy of the US dollar. Also, the government's control of the digital currency will allow it to combat money laundering, banking fraud and the financing of terrorist activities.

As I started discussing all these trends with my colleagues, it was clear that we needed to work out what they meant at an operational level.

* * *

So after surveying the landscape from a strategic fifty thousand feet, I descended to an operational fifty feet. In doing so, I had four fortuitous encounters that helped me map out the way forward for Eastnets. One of these happened as we were coming to terms with the fallout of the NSA hacking story. Luay Gadallah, newly appointed as Eastnets' chief technology officer, came to see me. He presented me with the estimated costs of putting everything back together again. They were enormous. Particularly high were the likely payments for new hardware systems. He may have detected my furrowed brow. At any rate, he clearly realized that they were going to be unaffordable—and he came up with a solution: cloud computing. I was sold on the idea from day one. As Satya Nadella has observed, cloud computing "[allows] for elastic scaling up or down on a self-service, pay-as-you-go basis."[74] Within weeks, Anas Jaber, who runs Eastnets' service bureau, launched the company's migration to the cloud. We selected three providers: Microsoft Azure, Amazon Web Services and a private cloud provider for our SWIFT network. By moving to the cloud, we were able to free up resources and focus on new products that were needed by our clients.

But what kinds of products did we need to develop?

It was clear from our strategic review that our banking clients were facing an astonishing series of threats, including banking fraud, cyberattacks and money laundering. Nowadays, banks really have no option but to overhaul their legacy systems, invest in new technology, update their software, and hire compliance officers and data scientists. The United Nations estimates that criminals are now laundering between 2 percent and 5 percent of global gross domestic product every year—which puts the cost at somewhere between $800 billion and $2 trillion.[75] Meanwhile, individuals and institutions are regularly being blacklisted for various misdemeanors, and so banks are having to take extra precautions to ensure that they do not provide financial services to these newly blacklisted people and organizations.

For ten years, our anti-money laundering tools had protected hundreds of our banking clients. It soon became clear that my R&D taskforce, which is always innovating and dreaming up new products, would have to harness the power of three new technologies: data analytics, machine learning and blockchain. I came to this conclusion after three other fortuitous encounters.

The first of these took place in the United States.

We were hosting a roadshow in New York, promoting our suite of products to prospective clients. During the session, I learned that one of the attendees was a man called Gregory Coleman. Now, if you have seen *The Wolf of Wall Street*, the blockbuster movie starring Leonardo DiCaprio, or read the book on which it is based, then you'll know Mr. Coleman as the FBI agent who finally tracked down the rogue broker, Jordan Belfort. Played by Kyle Chandler in the movie, Mr. Coleman's remarkable achievement was based on years of painstaking detective work, drawing connections in a slow, manual way. I was introduced to him, we got talking, he was fascinated to hear about our anti-money laundering software, and by the end of our conversation, he had agreed to come and speak at Eastnets' annual conference in Amman. During his presentation, he revealed the many different tactics used by financial criminals to circumvent banks' security protection, praised our range of products (only half jokingly saying that they would have cut the time he had taken to catch the Wolf of Wall Street), and provided the spark we needed to start incorporating AI-powered data analytics into our solutions.

Another of these encounters took place as the world's banks came to terms with the consequences of the extraordinary cyberattack on Bangladesh's central bank, when criminals used fraudulent orders on the SWIFT payment system to steal $81 million. The money was sent to Rizal Commercial Banking Corp, a bank headquartered in Manila, the Philippines' capital. Pretty quickly, it vanished into the murky underworld of gambling and casinos, and was never seen again. This event prompted Pierre Bourgognon, a senior executive at one of our loyal customers, Wells Fargo, the US bank, to get in touch. He expressed concern about the growing number of bank robberies conducted by criminals who were able to stage enormous heists simply by pressing a few buttons on a computer keyboard rather than by pulling the trigger of a sawed-off shotgun. His concern was entirely understandable: SWIFT handles fifteen million financial messages every day and facilitates the cross-border transfer of $40 trillion. Mr. Bourgognon had a question for us: Could we develop not just an anti-money laundering product but also an anti-fraud product? This got us thinking, and soon one of our brightest engineers, Nezar Nassr, who was a specialist in AI, realized that we could apply predictive analytics and machine learning to Wells Fargo's vast archive of SWIFT's messages. As a result, he created Eastnets' first anti-fraud product, en.Safe-watch Paymentguard. This detects and intercepts suspicious activity in real time while reducing the incidence of false positives. It means that if banks receive a strange message—one that is not consistent with those messages logged in their archive—the payment is automatically rejected.

The third of these product-related encounters led to Eastnets embracing blockchain technology. I was having dinner with Jehad Alqawasme, an old friend who used to work for Eastnets and who now works for Oracle, the US multinational computer company. He was telling me how Oracle was using blockchain technology to help banks transfer documents between their branches in different countries. It sounded fascinating—and something we should consider adapting for our purposes. After listening to Jehad, I put him in touch with Deya, who spearheads our development of new products. Immediately, she came back with a proposal.

Blockchain technology shot to prominence with the early success of Bitcoin, the cryptocurrency which advocates have sometimes labeled "digital gold." But its broader value as a fast and transparent method of conducting transactions is now being exploited in many different ways. In essence, it is a form of distributed ledger technology, where the key component is a digital ledger that links authenticated records of transactions—known as "blocks"—in a way that is transparent, trustworthy, verifiable, encrypted and immutable. Deya realized its value as a way of transporting vital information related to blacklisted people and organizations.

We have long had a partnership with Dow Jones' risk and compliance division, which helps companies comply with anti-money laundering, anti-bribery, corruption and economic sanction regulations in mitigating third-party risk. Before our latest blockchain innovation, Dow Jones used to send out updates of its sanctions watch list every eight hours. The trouble was that, with time zone differences, some banks risked serving people and organizations for several hours after they had been blacklisted.

Now, Dow Jones sends out the updated list, which contains some 2.4 million records, every hour, and we relay the information to banks within minutes with the help of Oracle's blockchain technology. It means that banks can meet their regulatory responsibilities, mitigate their risks, and avoid the damaging discovery that they are facilitating fraud, cybercrime, money laundering and terrorism.

* * *

As we rolled out these different AI-powered products, I began to consider what it meant for me and for everyone one at Eastnets—at a personal, individual level. What was the view from five feet? Just as I did so, news of a strange virus from China started to hit the headlines. I was in our Belgian offices when I first heard about COVID-19, and at the time, it was not clear how dangerous or how devastating on all of our lives it was going to be. But by mid-March 2020, as governments around the world started to introduce new lockdown measures, we resolved to close our offices and to institute a new work-from-home policy.

It was at this point that we thanked our lucky stars that we had migrated to the cloud. Of course, we had done so to provide a better service to our clients, but now it also meant that we could continue operating as if nothing had happened. And it meant that I could press ahead with my plan to get everyone ready for the digital future.

There is ample evidence to show that many companies fail to achieve their hoped-for benefits from ambitious digital transformation initiatives because they focus too much on the new technology and too little on the people who will have to use it on a day-to-day basis.[76] I did not want this to happen at Eastnets. So I ordered the development of an online training program for every single member of staff. I and my executive team enrolled in an INSEAD online program on "Strategy in the Age of Digital Disruption," led by Peter Zemsky, deputy dean of INSEAD and the Eli Lilly chaired professor of strategy and innovation; Eastnets' younger managers were sent on a digital marketing course; and everyone was given a primer on AI and data analytics.

I found these courses hugely valuable. Now in my mid-sixties, I am not a digital native. In fact, I amuse my colleagues when I tell them about my own technological journey. They can scarcely believe me when I tell them that I first saw a TV in 1965, when I was about ten years old. I was living in Amman at the time, and at about four or five o'clock every afternoon after school, I used to go with my friends to the local electronics store and watch *Tom & Jerry* cartoons broadcast on the TV standing in the shop window. But I have always believed that it is essential to keep learning, keep pressing forward, keep evolving. "Don't look back, unless it's a good view" is one of my mantras. Listen, read, observe, stay curious and don't stop asking questions—of others and of yourself. The more you do this, the more self-aware you become.

Why do I do what I do? This is a question that goes right to the heart of who I am and what Eastnets is. It is about my purpose and my company's purpose.

And it is a question that I try to answer next, in the final chapter of *Two Brown Envelopes*.

Chapter 14

WHY I DO WHAT I DO

THESE DAYS, MOST OF THE WORLD'S BIGGEST COMPANIES TALK about the importance of having a purpose—a raison d'être that goes beyond the pursuit of profit. The classic view, as expressed by the economist Milton Friedman, is that "there is one and only one social responsibility of business—to use its resources and engage in activities designed to increase its profits."[77] But in 2019, in a landmark decision, the Business Roundtable, which represents the chief executives of 181 of the world's largest companies, abandoned the long-standing view that "corporations exist principally to serve shareholders" and announced that "while each of our individual companies serves its own corporate purpose, we share a fundamental commitment to all of our stakeholders."[78]

About time, you might say.

But when you are an entrepreneur, running the company you founded, there is no need to confect a kind of nice-sounding, concocted purpose. In so many ways, the company is a part of you—it is the corporate manifestation of you. Or at least, it should be. It is often said that venture capitalists know whether to invest in a company by looking not at the account book but at the demeanor of the entrepreneur. What makes them tick? What gets them out of bed in the morning? If the answer is "I want to make a million dollars," then the investors may sensibly choose to withhold their money. If, on the other hand, the answer is "I want to catch and capitalize on the next opportunity," then they may just be persuaded to part with their cash.

I, for one, know few successful entrepreneurs who are primarily motivated by money. If you are only worried about the size of your paycheck, then you're probably better off trying to climb the corporate ladder of a publicly listed company. Yes, of course, money is important. In the Middle East, where there is no welfare state, no safety net, there is no alternative but to find ways to provide for oneself, one's family, one's community. In the early years of my entrepreneurial life, and at other points when I faced mounting debts and flirted with bankruptcy, I certainly felt the painful absence of money most acutely. But the solution was never to search for the next dollar. The solution was to search for the next idea, the next product, the next connection, the next opportunity. In my view, money is the by-product of a successful, purpose-driven company—not the other way round.

So to return to the question I posed in the previous chapter, Why do I do what I do? And by extension, why does Eastnets do what it does? In essence, as I will relay in this chapter, I and my company are driven by the desire to give people the tools to connect with each other and to participate in the global economy. But first, it is necessary to explain what shaped, and continues to shape, my thinking: my family upbringing, my Islamic faith and my far-reaching globalism.

* * *

If you came back with me to my family home in Jordan where I grew up, you would be immediately struck by an enormous, and very arresting, mural. Commissioned by my father and painted by one of my mother's brothers, it depicted a powerful scene in the life of Spartacus, the gladiator-slave who led a rebel army that stood up to the might of the Roman empire. I am sure, looking back, that the image drew inspiration from Kirk Douglas' chisel-jawed portrayal of the Thracian hero in the Hollywood blockbuster *Spartacus*. In one memorable scene in the movie, reflected in the mural, Spartacus prepares to meet his fate when a Roman centurion offers the defeated rebels to avoid death by crucifixion if they identify "the body or the living person of the slave called Spartacus." Bravely, he stood up, but before he could speak, a second slave jumps up and cries out, "I'm Spartacus." Then a third. Then a fourth. Until the whole rebel army rallies to Spartacus' side.

To me, this mural conveyed so much of what my father inculcated in me during my formative years: stand up for what you believe in, cooperate with others, don't shirk your responsibilities, work hard. As I explained in the first chapter, my father was jailed for speaking up for the rights of workers, for the cooperative movement and for the interests of the local community. It was thanks to him that I learned from a young age about the importance of being part of something bigger than yourself.

He taught me to be proud of my roots. The tragic history of Palestine loomed large in my childhood. How could it not? I was born on May 15—the anniversary of *Nakba*, the "catastrophe," when Palestinians were forced from their homeland after the creation of Israel. Also, he taught me to be proud of my Islamic faith. Growing up, I remember being surrounded by verses from the Qur'an. I know that he and my mother drew inspiration from the teachings of the holy book. The very first word revealed in the Qur'an is *iqra* or "read," and I was encouraged to explore the world through literature as soon as I could walk. Other powerful Qur'anic words are *jawda, ihsan* and *itqan*— referring to quality, perfection and continuous improvement. Work hard, persevere, help others, strive to the best of your ability—these were some of the messages that have stayed with me. One hadith left a particular impression on me: "Allah loves if one of you does a job to perfect it." In other words, whatever you do, do it well.

As well as my upbringing and my faith, it was my early introduction to the wider world that shaped me and my company. Of course, as a Palestinian and a Muslim, I am a member of two very global communities. The Palestinian diaspora is extraordinary. Indeed, my own family is a kind of commonwealth of nations. I, personally, have dual Jordanian and Belgian citizenship; I have one brother who is American, another who is Australian, and a sister who is Jordanian; and my son was born in Bulgaria, and his children—my grandchildren—are British. Likewise, the Islamic faith ranges across national borders, connecting diverse communities. Alongside these inherited global links, I was brought up as a citizen of the world. Born in Saudi Arabia, I was educated in Jordan (at a French school),

Kuwait, England and Bulgaria. Then I worked for a German company (Siemens) and an American company (in Florida).

Naturally, as I moved from country to country, I learned to adapt, I learned to appreciate not only the differences between cultures but also the *similarities* between them. Above all, I learned to listen. So often, people assume that communication is all about speaking. Actually, half of the time, it's about listening. In the 1970s, when I was living in England, one of my favorite singers was Cat Stevens, the British pop star who later converted to Islam and took the name Yusuf Islam. His song "Father and Son" really resonated with me. It tells the story of a father who does not understand his son's desire to forge out on his own and a son who struggles to articulate his wish to break free. There is one crucial line: "From the moment I could talk / I was ordered to listen."

I, too, was not so much ordered as *encouraged* to listen by my father. And as I have traveled between cultures, this has served me well throughout my life. When I first went to the United States in 1982, I was truly shocked by how Americans were so direct and seemingly abrasive. At first, I took it for rudeness. It was only later that I came to realize that everybody spoke in this unvarnished way. When they *said* something, they *meant* it. I was so unused to this. Although I had enjoyed a cosmopolitan upbringing, I had nevertheless been steeped in a culture of politeness that encouraged conversations laced with concealed meanings. Erin Meyer, an INSEAD professor, puts this wonderfully in her book *The Culture Map*.[79] She draws a distinction between "low-context cultures" such as those in the United States and UK, where the expectation is that you say what you mean, and "high-context cultures" such as those across the Middle East (and Japan), where so much communication takes place in the way things are said. One of my favorite writers is Khalil Gibran, the Lebanese-born American writing in the first half of the twentieth century, and he expressed this hidden world with marvelous precision: "Between what is said and not meant, and what is meant and not said, most of love is lost."

* * *

In a sense, my family upbringing, Islamic faith and far-reaching global experience provided the perfect apprenticeship for an entrepreneur in today's fast-globalizing world. My company, Eastnets, reflects these early influences. It is diverse, cosmopolitan and enlightened, with employees from twenty-four countries, located in ten offices around the world. English is the language of the business—whether you are in Amman, Belgium, Dubai or New Jersey—and we have developed what Professor Meyer describes as the kind of "low-context" culture that is necessary in a multicultural setting.

Together, as a company, we are engaged in a common purpose: to connect people with each other and to the global economy. This has been my mission since the first day I launched my company, and while I think my business has evolved through three distinct phases—as I will now explain—I consider that they are all linked by this one unifying common purpose.

The first phase was from 1984–1990. When I came back from the United States, I was inspired to launch the Jordan Computer Center by the idea of the democratization of technology—the idea that anyone, whoever they are, can harness the power of personal computers. I wanted to give Jordanians the same chance to buy computers as the Americans I had seen in Florida and, in this way, to connect to each other and the rest of the world. When my showroom business faced competition from my former partners, I switched to distributing the pioneering Sakhr MSX Arab-English edutainment console. Again, this was about giving young Jordanians the chance to learn English, the international *lingua franca*, and thereby acquire the skills they needed to converse in the world around them. Every now and then, even after all these years, I encounter people who come up to me and say how much they treasured their Sahkr MSX console—and how much of a role it played in their early life. This really gives me a thrill, I can tell you.

The second evolutionary phase was from 1991–2008. After the first Gulf War, which triggered the collapse of my computer business, I created what was, on the face of it, a completely different business: linking banks to central networks. At first, there were small deals that revolved around phone banking. The breakthrough came when I started providing banks with access to SWIFT. This allowed banks to offer their services to more people—and it allowed me to continue with my mission to connect more people to the global economy. Over the next few years, the idea of financial inclusion was a powerful driver for what became Eastern Networks and then Eastnets. I was able to expand the business beyond Jordan and become a multiregional company.

During this period, Eastnets connected many relatively poor countries to SWIFT and, through this, to the global economy. I have previously mentioned some of the countries: Afghanistan,

Libya, Yemen. The one I left out earlier in my book, and reserved for here, is the occupied Palestinian territories—the West Bank and Gaza Strip. Throughout my life, I have harbored hopes that the international community would one day implement the countless UN resolutions supporting the creation of an independent Palestinian nation-state. During my student years in England, I was an activist. During the 1990s, after the signing of the Oslo Accords, which paved the way for Palestinian self-rule, I was heavily involved in the preparations for establishing an independent state, advising on the financial and banking requirements. But these efforts ended with the second Palestinian *Intifada*, or uprising, which drew criticism from around the world (unlike the first *Intifada* of 1987, which elicited worldwide sympathy). I was left to ponder how best I could help the cause. My opportunity came in the mid-2000s. I put the Palestinian central bank on SWIFT and, not only that, gave the territories their own distinct digital identity: PS. Until then, its code was shared with Israel. It may have been a small victory. But it felt symbolically important.

The third phase started in 2008, and although the business has evolved considerably since then, it has broadly retained the same broad vision. It was in 2008 that Eastnets acquired SIDE International and, with one big leap, became what I call an IP company—a company with its own intellectual property. Suddenly, we were able to offer banks a range of anti-money-laundering and other services that would protect them and their customers. In the past fifteen years, cybercrime has grown exponentially. The digital tools designed to connect people have been weaponized by financial hackers, criminals and state-backed operatives. So, just as we have always tried to give people the tools that they need to connect with each other and to participate in the global economy, we now also try to safeguard them when they use those tools.

* * *

Jordan Computer Center, Eastern Networks, Eastnets—the name may have changed over the years, but the company's central mission hasn't. For nearly forty years, it has focused on giving people the tools to connect with each other and to participate in the global economy, and this common purpose has driven the approach to charitable work too. Over the years, I and Eastnets have supported two major philanthropic initiatives. One was Net Ketabi—literally "net book" in Arabic. This program was designed to provide around 280,000 children in the occupied Palestinian territories with their own computers. The program was innovative because rather than simply donating the computers, it encouraged the children (and their families) to buy the computers, albeit with the help of generously funded microfinance support. We raised money for the program, which won the backing of Intel, through its charitable Intel World Ahead foundation, PalTel, the Palestinian Investment Fund, the Skoll Foundation, and individuals such as Anousheh Ansari, an American Iranian entrepreneur and the first woman space tourist, with whom I served on the Net Ketabi advisory board. One year, I took a team of Eastnets' employees to the foothills of the Himalayas, where we hiked and raised a significant sum of money that was channeled into the fund.[80]

The other initiative, which remains very close to my heart, is the work of the Rewell Society.[81] Originally called the Rehabilitation and Welfare Society, it was founded nearly thirty years ago by my father. It is animated by his belief that it is better to give people the tools for succeeding in the long term than to dole out cash to them for spending in the short term. Once they have the skills, they never lose them. If they have some cash handouts, they soon come back for more. My father wanted to help people to help themselves—to stand on their own two feet. And so do I. After my father's death, I took over responsibility for the charity and incorporated it into Eastnets' charitable activities. Every year, the company contributes to the fund, and many employees pledge a portion of their annual salary to the society.

To date, Rewell has provided more than forty thousand poor and underprivileged Jordanians with vocational skills, giving them the essential tools to succeed in this fast-changing world. In recent years, there has been a particular focus on helping women in the Jordan valley—in particular, supporting entrepreneurial projects related to farming activities such as cattle-rearing and beehive management. This took on greater importance during the lockdown associated with the global coronavirus pandemic. Beehive management is a critical part of the local ecosystem: the bees not only produce honey but also facilitate the pollination of crops in the valley. Normally, the hives are moved from the valley floor to higher ground, where the bees can avoid the heat of summer and pollinate new crops. But this all but stopped at the start of the lockdown, devastating the local population of bees and threatening to damage the local economy. As a result, the Rewell Society has stepped in with a package of support: offering services to enable the women to move their hives to higher ground and supplying flour for bread-making to tide them over until they can be self-sufficient again.

Through this kind of activity, we seek to inspire individuals and local communities. By the same token, we do, ourselves, draw inspiration. I still enthuse about the trip to the Himalayas, and I still get excited when I recall how I completed the London-Paris bike ride—which I did at the instigation of Jaap Kamp, Eastnets' former chairman, and which raised money for Action Medical, a London charity.

But there is nothing more exciting than seeing someone we have supported develop a new skill, build a business and get the confidence to take off in new directions. There is nothing more thrilling than to see someone seize the opportunity we have given them.

* * *

Long ago, my father sat me down in his office in Kuwait. He laid out two brown envelopes on his desk. It looked as if he was going to offer me a choice. Actually, he didn't offer me a choice at all. That's because he had already offered me any number of opportunities during the previous twenty years—and I had squandered pretty much all of them. He gave me an envelope with a few dollars, and said, in effect, "Take it, or leave it." I took it, of course. Also, from that day to this, I took every opportunity that came my way.

When your back is up against the wall, it focuses the mind—it really does. Little by little, with each new opportunity, I began to articulate the purpose of my company. I didn't invent it in one inspirational lightbulb moment. I didn't manufacture it for some glossy marketing brochure. It evolved as a response to my customers—listening to them, hearing what they had to say, working out how to solve their problems and satisfy their needs.

Today, I am happy to say why I do what I do: to connect people, to protect them and their assets and to empower them to participate in the global economy.

Conclusion

THE EIGHT SECRETS FOR BOUNCING BACK FROM FAILURE

I<small>F YOU LOOK ALONG THE SHELVES OF YOUR LOCAL BOOKSTORE</small> or, more likely, scroll through the dust jackets on Amazon, you will find any number of volumes on how to achieve success, how to "own" it, how to be number one. But, as I hope I have explained in this book, there are no shortcuts to success, no easy one-two-three, no substitute for launching your own business and learning as you go along. And when you do summon the courage to launch your company, you must expect not only to enjoy the sweet taste of success but also the bitterness of failure after failure after failure. How you deal with those dark moments will determine how ultimately successful you will be.

It was to convey this message that caused me to write this book. Throughout, I have tried to reflect on what were often challenging experiences and record some of the lessons I took away from each one. Now, at the end of the book, I want to summarize what

I consider to be the key takeaways.

If you ask me for my tips for bouncing back from failure, I can reel off eight of them, starting with the ability to join the dots.

1. Join the Dots

The French word "entrepreneur" is a conjunction of two words: "entre" and "preneur." Together, they describe an action-man or action-woman, someone who "undertakes" to do something, who gets things done. But the first word, "entre," is interesting. On its own, it can mean "between." And in the context of the entrepreneur, that is significant.

In my experience, an entrepreneur is someone who not only undertakes to do something but also stands like a bridge between things, making connections, joining the dots, bringing disparate ideas together.

This is what I have done all my life.

In a way, I am, as a Palestinian exile, inured to a life of being in the middle, between things. I was born in Saudi Arabia, have joint Jordanian-Belgian citizenship, spent significant amounts of my youth in Kuwait, England and Bulgaria, briefly toyed with emigrating to Canada, and now live in Dubai.

And from my earliest business ventures, I have sought to bring disparate worlds together. While I was still a student, I connected a Kuwaiti and a Bulgarian, who had a shared interest in German-designed forklift trucks. Then, when I launched the first computer store in Jordan, I acted as a reseller, linking customers with PC manufacturers. Later, I started what I still run today—a networks business which, by definition, makes connections. This business really took off when I had the serendipitous conversation on a Cyprus beach: my interlocutor had developed SWIFT software for PCs, and I, through my banking clients, knew that small- and medium-sized financial institutions in the Middle East would jump at the chance of using SWIFT for a fraction of the usual cost.

And so it has continued. Today, I remain on the lookout for gaps in the market which I can bridge by making the right connections.

2. Don't Be Afraid to Make Mistakes (But Don't Make the Same Mistake Twice)

Few companies tolerate failure. In these highly competitive times, CEOs tend to be impatient with people who underperform on a routine basis. Yet, ironically, some of the world's most successful entrepreneurs say they have learned more from their failures than their successes. In other words, if they hadn't in some way "failed," they wouldn't be where they are today. Take Jeff Bezos, founder of Amazon. He is on record as saying that as well as posting many successes, his company has endured "billions of dollars of failures" along the way.[82] Meanwhile, his rival for the title of world's richest man, Elon Musk, who runs Tesla and SpaceX, has tweeted, "If things are not failing, you are not innovating enough."[83]

So failure is an option. In their book *The Wisdom of Failure*, Laurence G. Weinzimmer and Jim McConoughey observe that "real failure doesn't come from making mistakes; rather, it comes from avoiding errors at all possible cost, from the fear of taking risks to the inability to grow." For the avoidance of doubt, they add, "Being mistake-free is not success."[84]

I couldn't agree more.

Equally, it is important to learn from failure. If you make the same mistake twice, then you really have failed. I certainly know that I have made many mistakes in my life, but on each occasion, I found a way to develop new ways of thinking and new ways of doing things differently—and better.

3. Be Positive

Everything has a solution. I really believe this. Even seemingly intractable problems have a workaround.

"Do you sleep well at night?" my father once asked me, when I was fighting to clear my name from the Interpol list.

"I sleep very well," I replied. Of course, I bore full responsibility for my mistakes. But I knew things would turn out okay. Somehow, I just knew it.

I am, by nature, an optimist. For me, the cup is always half full, never half empty. I think that entrepreneurs have to have this sunny outlook on life. In business, there are so many obstacles that are put in your way that if you, yourself, become another obstacle through the negative way you think about things, then you will never succeed.

There is a Qur'anic verse that has always inspired me on this subject: "So, verily, with every difficulty there is relief." To put it another way, every cloud has a silver lining. If you believe this, as I do, then you will do your best to be positive and—just as important—project that positivity to those around you. If, as a founder-entrepreneur, you look downcast, that sense of depression will spread through your home and your office like wildfire. If, by contrast, you look upbeat, then that mood of positivity will be shared by your family, your colleagues and your customers.

4. Seek Advice from Trusted Advisors

You cannot build a business on your own. Many of the world's great businesses were created by a double act. Think Rolls-Royce (Charles Rolls and Henry Royce), Procter & Gamble (William Procter and James Gamble) and Hewlett-Packard (Bill Hewlett and David Packard) or Microsoft (Bill Gates and Paul Allen), Apple (Steve Jobs and Steve Wozniak) and Google (Larry Page and Sergey Brin). But if, like me, you didn't start with a business partner, then you must seek out advice from friends, family and other people you trust.

In my early years, I had all the brashness of youth and ignored the counsel of my family and friends, and I paid a heavy price when the first Gulf War began. Since then, I have tried to surround myself with a network of people whose opinion I trust—and to listen to them (although, of course, I make the final decisions and take responsibility for them too). Until he passed away, my father was my lighthouse. I knew that if I ever strayed too far from what he advised—or what I thought he would have done if he were in my shoes—I was in trouble. Also, in my early years, while I was still finding my feet as an entrepreneur, Mohammed Al-Sharekh was a valued advisor.

These men are more properly called mentors: people you look up to, learn from and, in some way, imitate. But you also need to draw on the wisdom of the people who you spend time with—in particular, your colleagues, the people who share with you the highs and lows of doing business. In her book *Culture Map*, Erin Meyer draws a distinction between "cognitive trust," the trust that "comes from the head" and is "based on the confidence you feel in another person's accomplishments, skills, and reliability," and "affective trust," the trust that "comes from the heart" and "arises from feelings of emotional closeness, empathy, or friendship."[85] I have developed strong cognitive and affective trust relationships with two of my colleagues: Fahed Abu Higleh and Deya Innab. They have been valued sounding boards for many years.

But you should take extra special care when giving responsibility to people who control your company's financial affairs. In an entrepreneurial business, you come to rely heavily on your key executives, and it can be easy to let personal relationships cloud your judgement. I was particularly reliant on one of my senior executives when I was fighting to clear my name and obliged to reside in Jordan. When, after nearly four years, I was able to resume my normal pattern of working, I uncovered a multimillion-dollar black hole in the company accounts. I was left to rue the day I trusted one person to be in charge of the company's finances.

5. Be Dynamic—Always on the Move

Stay forward-looking. Never rest on your laurels. Never be completely satisfied, because this can quickly evolve into complacency—and complacency is the death rattle for any business. Necessarily, to be dynamic, you need to take risks, calculated risks. As Garry Kasparov, the great chess champion, once said, "If you don't take risks, you don't drink champagne." In chess, of course, you have to move when it's your turn. In his playing days, Kasparov was an advocate of seizing the initiative because "the attacker always has the advantage" and the resulting proactive position "puts positive pressure on you while challenging your competition."[86] In the language of business, this is translated as "first-mover advantage."

Time and again, I have been ultraconscious of making a move—whether or not it is my turn. After the first Gulf War, I switched from selling computers to selling solutions such as phone banking, national ID cards and bank networking software for personal computers. Then I switched again to a partnership with SWIFT, which opened an extraordinarily wide range of new opportunities. And then, as I faced another crisis after failing to sell Eastnets to an Italian rival, I moved quickly to buy SIDE International, hurriedly raising the capital, arranging a bridging loan and convincing the owners to sell the business.

In the wake of the COVID-19 pandemic, which has accelerated the pace of technological change, the capacity to be dynamic, agile and ready to change direction at a moment's notice will be more important than ever.

6. Develop a Panoptic View

It is imperative that you constantly seek new perspectives on what you are doing. To do this, read widely, travel far, and be open and receptive to new things, new influences, new possibilities.

When I was at school, my science teacher taught me about Professor C. V. Raman, an Indian physicist who, in the early 1920s, contested the established view articulated by the great nineteenth-century British physicist Lord Rayleigh that "the much-admired dark blue of the deep sea has nothing to do with the color of water but is simply the blue of the sky seen by reflection." Putting this view to the test, he carried out some experiments and showed that this view could not possibly be true.[87]

From this, I first learned that it was important to be curious and to never assume that what you were told was correct. Sakichi Toyoda, the founder of Toyota, once said that it is important to "ask 'why' five times about every matter."[88] I fully agree.

7. Be Diverse

Early on, I learned that you run too many risks if you do not spread your bets. Ever since then, I have sought to develop diverse products and services, operate in a diverse set of markets, and promote diverse teams of people (who typically make better, more informed decisions). I was probably influenced, at least subliminally, by Antoine de Saint-Exupéry. I came across his *Le Petit Prince* when I attended a French school in Jordan. I have since reread his wonderful novella, and there is a sentence that really resonates with me: *Soyez curieux et vivez des experiences diverse!* "Be curious and live diverse experiences!"[89]

Of course, there is always the danger that you spread yourself too thin. There is certainly a balance to be struck between efficiency and effectiveness. In 2008, I remember a fierce debate around the boardroom table in the aftermath of the financial crisis. One of Eastnets' cost-conscious shareholders advocated shutting down the company's SWIFT service bureau. I thought this was shortsighted. I argued that the banks, facing their own cash crisis, would want to outsource their financial messaging operation. As things turned out, I was right, and Eastnets prospered. But if I had not won the argument, who knows what would have happened.

8. Believe in Yourself

If you don't, no one else will. There will be times when nothing seems to go right, when the gloom is unremitting, when there is no sign of light at the end of the tunnel. But believe me, if you believe in yourself, you can overcome the biggest setbacks.

A key part of believing in yourself is *being yourself.* Authenticity is critical to success. It breeds respect and trust. Yes, of course, you should admire other people—their achievements, their successes. But don't try to *be* them, don't try to be someone else, someone you're not. Because when you're down, your mask will slip.

Indeed, it is often when you are at your lowest point that you find out who you really are and what you're made of. If, as an entrepreneur, you are doing your job properly, there are many such moments when you are forced to face an uncomfortable truth or deal with the painful consequences of your actions.

I've been there, and pulled through, because I believed that I could do it.

* * *

I don't have a simple formula for success. I don't know anyone who does (although I know many people who claim they do). I do, however, have a formula for learning the lessons of failure.

Ultimately, failure is the most common experience of the entrepreneur. Those who overcome it, they survive. Those who don't, don't.

The eight takeaways from my life as an entrepreneur are things that I have learned the hard way. I now take great pleasure in passing them on—in speeches, MBA classes, lectures and now this book.

I know, of course, that there is no substitute for learning these lessons from the real lived experience of failure. When running a business, there is no easy way.

But hopefully, if you are an aspiring entrepreneur, you will get some reassurance and draw some inspiration when you find yourself, as you surely will, facing your equivalent of my father's two brown envelopes.

ACKNOWLEDGMENTS

As you will know by now, I am something of a movie buff, and I often like to draw parallels between Hollywood blockbusters and real life. Here's another parallel: when the credits roll at the end of a movie, it never ceases to amaze me how many people are involved in its creation. I now realize that, in this respect, books are like films, and so I would like to finish *Two Brown Envelopes* with the book equivalent of rolling credits.

I would like to thank Dr. Simon Targett, a former associate editor of the *Financial Times*, who has helped me craft this book, weaving my stories, memories and ideas into a polished manuscript.

I would like to thank several people who have kindly read the manuscript at different stages over the past year and given me hugely valuable thoughts, guidance and feedback: Deya Innab, David Salloum, Professor Ian Woodward and Dr. H.E. Fawaz Zu'bi.

I would like to thank Roger Jones, who has long been my adviser on marketing and introduced me to Simon. I would like to thank

Shatha Ariqat, my long-time assistant, who has helped keep everything on track.

I would like to thank Professor Stephen Meziah from INSEAD. He cowrote the first case study on Eastnets, and he gave me the chance to present it to various cohorts of INSEAD's MBA and executive students over many years and in many different locations. I would also like to thank Charlotte Mason, also of INSEAD, for inviting me to speak at her MBA startup bootcamps in Fontainebleau and Madrid. The chance to speak with and get feedback from INSEAD's wonderful MBA and executive students helped me shape my thoughts for this book.

Everyone at Scribe Media has been incredibly professional. In particular, I would like to thank Holly Gorman, Rikki Jump and Becca Kadison.

And now to my biggest debts of gratitude: to my family and my extended family at Eastnets.

I would like to thank all my colleagues at Eastnets—those who are now taking the company forward and those who helped build the company over the past forty years and who have since moved on to other ventures. You have stood by me through thick and thin. My appreciation and pride in everything you do is boundless.

I would like to thank my son, Amir, and my grandchildren, whom I have not seen since the start of the COVID-19 pandemic. Your unlimited love continues to inspire me.

Acknowledgments

Above all, I would like to thank my wife, Hanin, and my daughters, Joud, Masa and Nour. Throughout the various lockdowns that we have all endured over the past eighteen months, you have been unbelievably patient and forgiving as I worked to complete *Two Brown Envelopes*. You know that I couldn't have done any of it without you.

ENDNOTES

1 Edward Said, *Reflections on Exile and Other Literary and Cultural Essays* (London: Granta, 2000), p. 186.

2 "Communication Received from United Kingdom Delegation Concerning Palestine Government Scholars, and Palestine Government Officers Attending Courses of Instruction outside Palestine," United Nations Palestine Commission, April 2, 1948: https://unispal.un.org/DPA/DPR/unispal.nsf/0/C06F55B36213BE1585257098006DD4CE

3 Aramco, *Energy to the World: The Story of Saudi Aramco* (Houston, Texas: Aramco Services Company, 2011), vol. 1, pp. 196, 199: https://www.aramco.com/-/media/publications/books/energytotheworldvol1english.pdf; and Madawi Al-Rasheed, A History of Saudi Arabia, 2nd ed. (Cambridge: Cambridge University Press, 2010), pp. 99–100.

4 "Mohammed Ayyash Mulhim (1927-2015): A Life of Advocacy & Charity," Rewell Society: https://www.rewellsociety.org/about-us

5 *Aramco, Energy to the World*, vol. 1, p. 168: https://www.aramco.com/-/media/publications/books/energytotheworldvol1english.pdf; and Al-Rasheed, *A History of Saudi Arabia*, pp. 92–96.

6 "Aramco Confirms Oil Labor Strife," New York Times, October 20, 1953: https://www.nytimes.com/1953/10/20/archives/aramco-confirms-oil-labor-strife-13000-saudi-arabians-strike-after.html

7 Aramco, *Energy to the World*, vol. 1, p. 185.

8 "Bill Gates Discusses His Lifelong Love of Books and Reading," *Time*, May 22, 2017: https://time.com/4786837/bill-gates-books-reading/

9 Oliver Wendell Holmes Sr., *The Autocrat of the Breakfast-Table* (Boston, 1958), Chapter XI.

10 "The Hall," Gray's Inn website: https://www.graysinn.org.uk/history/the-hall

11 Yasser Arafat's speech to the UN, November 13, 1974, para. 57: https://unispal.un.org/DPA/DPR/unispal.nsf/0/A238EC7A3E13EED18525624A007697EC

12 Aramco, *Energy to the World*, vol. 1, p. 196: https://www.aramco.com/-/media/publications/books/energytotheworldvol1english.pdf

13 For this history, see: Bob Hakewill, "Brooke House" (April 2009): https://resources.finalsite.net/images/v1578995906/brookehousecom/mkuwo1leeujqfdmpmgaq/the-elms.pdf

14 Yasser Araft's speech to the UN, November 13, 1974, paragraph 82: https://unispal.un.org/DPA/DPR/unispal.nsf/0/A238EC7A3E13EED18525624A007697EC

15 United Nations Resolution 3236 (XXIX) Question of Palestine, November 22, 1974: https://undocs.org/A/RES/3236%20(XXIX). Also: "The Question of Palestine and the General Assembly," United Nations website: https://www.un.org/unispal/data-collection/general-assembly/

16 For the history, see: "Farewell to campus," *BBC Local Northampton*, November 14, 2006: http://www.bbc.co.uk/northamptonshire/content/articles/2006/11/13/farewell_to_campus_feature.shtml

17 For information, see: http://alsharekhcollection.com/about-us/; and https://medium.com/@Mussaad/caught-between-a-rock-and-a-hard-place-the-sad-story-of-sakhr-2f06961e22f8

18 "Life Bleak for Jordanians Who Fled Kuwait," *New York Times*, June 25, 1991: https://www.nytimes.com/1991/06/25/world/life-bleak-for-jordanians-who-fled-kuwait.html

19 "Charting A Difficult Course: Jordan In The 1950s," Office of King Hussein I: http://kinghussein.gov.jo/his_periods1.html

20 "HID to Acquire Fargo Electronics," *Secure ID News*, May 23, 2006: https://www.secureidnews.com/news-item/hid-to-acquire-fargo-electronics/

21 For the history of INSEAD, see: https://www.insead.edu/about/who-we-are

22 INSEAD, "Advanced Management Program": https://www.insead.edu/executive-education/general-management/advanced-management-programme

23 Bolero, "Company Overview": https://www.bolero.net/company-overview/;; and "Bolero: History of the Bolero Project and the International Group of P&I Clubs (the Group) Cover," *UKP&I*, September 30, 2010: https://www.ukpandi.com/news-and-resources/circulars/2010/bolero-history-of-the-bolero-project-and-the-international-group-of-pi-clubs-the-groupcover/

Endnotes

24 "Tread Lightly Along the New Silk Road," *Financial Times*, January 29, 2007: https://www.ft.com/content/f67992ae-afd5-11db-94ab-0000779e2340

25 "BizTalk Accelerator for SWIFT Automates Three out of Four Messages and Saves $100,000 for Turkish Bank," Microsoft BizTalk Server Customer Solution Case Study (Microsoft Corporation, 2004): https://media-expl.licdn.com/dms/document/C4D2DAQHhxXr-EQfazg/profile-treasury-document-pdf-analyzed/0/1602221254911?e=1630778400&v=beta&t=qt2nQpVMNcM5f5J1LqTYnkJ1ufBRl-CxleJNk03lR6uY

26 "Ali Bujsaim Interview: Meet the Emirati World Cup Referee Who Kept Stoichkov and Ronaldo in Check," *The National*, June 11, 2018: https://www.thenational-news.com/sport/football/ali-bujsaim-interview-meet-the-emirati-world-cup-refer-ee-who-kept-stoichkov-and-ronaldo-in-check-1.738825

27 "Eastnets Uses Zebra Card Printers to Produce Contactless Smart Cards at Dubai International Airport," *Source Security*: https://www.sourcesecurity.com/news/co-2260-ga.155.html

28 "Counterparty Link Raises the Bar For Counterparty, Entity Data," A-Team Insight, February 1, 2005: https://a-teaminsight.com/counterparty-link-rais-es-the-bar-for-counterparty-entity-data/?brand=rti; "EastNets to carry Counterpar-tyLink entity data," FinExtra, 22 February, 2008: https://www.finextra.com/pressar-ticle/20040/eastnets-to-carry-counterpartylink-entity-data

29 "Not an Oscar, even better EastNets Egypt wins the CPL Annual Quality Awards (#AQUA) - Quality is what we are about," Facebook, February 4, 2014: https://www.facebook.com/photo/?fbid=588737224548332&set=not-an-oscar-even-better-eastnets-egypt-wins-the-cpl-annual-quality-awards-aqua-

30 "NCH Group: Software for Automatic Banking," *Discover Bologna* (Promo Bologna, n.d.), p. 31: https://silo.tips/download/discover-bologna-where-quali-ty-of-life-entrepreneurship-and-culture-meet-italy-s

31 "TAS Tecnologia Avanzata dei Sistemi S.p.A. N.C.H. Group: Appointment of Ingegner Giuseppe Caruso as Chief Executive Officer," TAS S.p.A., press release, September 11, 2006.

32 For IFC's announcement, see "Eastnets Secures Investment from IFC," *Arabian Business*, November 11, 2008: https://www.arabianbusiness.com/eastnets-se-cures-investment-from-ifc-83183.html

33 For Eastnets' statement, see: "Eastnets Get Cash Injection from IFC," Emirates 24/7, November 9, 2008: https://www.emirates247.com/eb247/banking-finance/is-lamic-finance/eastnets-gets-cash-injection-from-ifc-2008-11-09-1.230657

34 For the Chartis Research list, see: https://www.chartis-research.com/finan-cial-risk-and-evaluation/credit-risk/risktech100-2009-212

35   For the announcement of the Chartis Research report and the IBS Publishing news, see: https://www.bobsguide.com/guide/news/2009/Dec/14/eastnets-receives-high-ranking-in-chartis-risktech100-survey/

36   "Global Investors Keen on Acquiring Eastnets," Emirates 24/7, December 8, 2009: https://www.emirates247.com/eb247/economy/uae-economy/global-investors-keen-on-acquiring-eastnets-2009-12-08-1.22180

37   For details of the acquisition, see "Gulf: Ambition Usurps Domestic Focus," *Financial Times*, September 9, 2009: https://www.ft.com/content/9a03a1dc-9cdf-11de-ab58-00144feabdc0; and U.S. Securities & Exchange Commission, "Acquisitions. 12 Months Ended Dec. 31, 2011": https://www.sec.gov/Archives/edgar/data/1011006/000119312512086972/R11.htm

38   World Economic Forum, *Annual Report 2009–2010*, p. 8: http://www3.weforum.org/docs/WEF_AnnualReport_2009-10.pdf

39   "Mobile Remittances: Secure, Compliant Mobile Money Transfer," Eastnets, December 4, 2011: https://www.slideshare.net/EastNets/eastnets-enmore

40   For the details of the patent, see: https://patents.justia.com/inventor/hazem-mohamed-mulhim

41   Mohamad S. Fakhreddin and Stephen J. Mezias, EastNets: *Opportunity In Every Difficulty* (INSEAD, February 5, 2012).

42   "Hazem Mulhim: World Banks Trust This Man!" *Fortune Arabia*, April 4, 2012.

43   "Abu Dhabi Quietly Cashes Out of Barclays," Financial Times, July 18, 2013: https://www.ft.com/content/aa25ecb8-efc0-11e2-a237-00144feabdc0

44   "Why Are Some of the World's Biggest Banks Leaving the UAE?" *Arabian Business*, February 13, 2015: https://www.arabianbusiness.com/why-are-some-of-world-s-biggest-banks-leaving-uae--582005.html

45   Michael D. Watkins, *The First 90 Days: Proven Strategies for Getting Up to Speed Faster and Smarter*, updated edition (Boston, Massachusetts: Harvard Business Review Press, 2013), pp. 71–75.

46   T.E. Lawrence, *Seven Pillars of Wisdom* (London: Penguin Modern Classics, 2000), Chapter 75.

47   Haruki Murakami, *Kafka on the Shore. Translated from the Japanese by Philip Gabriel*. Kindle Edition (London: Vintage Books, 2011), p. 4.

48   "US Government 'Monitored Bank Transfers'," *BBC*, April 17, 2018: https://www.bbc.co.uk/news/technology-39606575

Endnotes

49 "Dubai Financial Services Bureau Eastnests Denies Claims of Hacking," The National, April 15, 2017: https://www.thenationalnews.com/business/dubai-financial-services-bureau-eastnets-denies-claims-of-hacking-1.86955

50 "Secrecy, Security, the President and the Press," *New York Times*, July 2, 2006: https://www.nytimes.com/2006/07/02/opinion/02pub-ed.html

51 "Bank Data Is Sifted by U.S. in Secret to Block Terror," *New York Times*, June 23, 2006: https://www.nytimes.com/2006/06/23/washington/23intel.html

52 "Bank Data Is Sifted by U.S. in Secret to Block Terror," *New York Times*, June 23, 2006: https://www.nytimes.com/2006/06/23/washington/23intel.html

53 "New York Times Stirs Controversy in Exposing Government Secrets," NPR, June 27, 2006: https://www.npr.org/transcripts/5515699?t=1612986180825

54 "Secrecy, Security, the President and the Press," *New York Times*.

55 Matt Suiche, "ShadowBrokers: The NSA Compromised the SWIFT Network," Comae Technologies, April 14, 2017: https://blog.comae.io/the-nsa-compromised-swift-network-50ec3000b195

56 The Office of Tailored Access Operations (TAO) is now called Computer Networks Operations.

57 "Hacking Group Claims N.S.A. Infiltrated Mideast Banking System," *New York Times*, April 15, 2017: https://www.nytimes.com/2017/04/15/us/shadow-brokers-nsa-hack-middle-east.html

58 "US Government 'Monitored Bank Transfers,'" *BBC*, April 16, 2017: https://www.bbc.co.uk/news/technology-39606575

59 Edward Snowden, "The Mother Of All Exploits escaped from an NSA laboratory and is wrecking the internet", *Twitter*, April 14, 2017: https://twitter.com/Snowden/status/853018715025281028; "MOAB Strike: US Military Defends Use Of Massive Bomb In Afghanistan," *BBC*, April 14, 2017: https://www.bbc.co.uk/news/world-asia-39603122

60 "Major Leak Suggests N.S.A. Was Deep in Middle East Banking System," *Wired*, April 14, 2017: https://www.wired.com/2017/04/major-leak-suggests-nsa-deep-middle-east-banking-system/

61 "N.S.A. Contractor Arrested in Possible New Theft of Secrets," *New York Times*, October 5, 2016: https://www.nytimes.com/2016/10/06/us/nsa-leak-booz-allen-hamilton.html

62 "Security Breach and Spilled Secrets Have Shaken the N.S.A. to Its Core," *New York Times,* November 12, 2017: https://www.nytimes.com/2017/11/12/us/nsa-shadow-brokers.html and "Hackers Hit Dozens of Countries Exploiting Stolen N.S.A.

Tool," *New York Times*, May 12, 2017: https://www.nytimes.com/2017/05/12/world/europe/uk-national-health-service-cyberattack.html

63   Ian C. Woodward, V. "Paddy" Padmanabhan, Sameer Hasija and Ram Charan, *The Phoenix Encounter Method: Lead Like Your Business Is on Fire* (New York: McGraw-Hill Education, 2021), p. 78.

64   Woodward et al., *The Phoenix Encounter Method*, p. 72.

65   Nicholas Davis, "What Is the Fourth Industrial Revolution," World Economic Forum, January 19, 2016: https://www.weforum.org/agenda/2016/01/what-is-the-fourth-industrial-revolution/

66   "The Bionic Company," Boston Consulting Group: https://www.bcg.com/en-gb/capabilities/digital-technology-data/bionic-company

67   Ian Goldin and Chris Kutarna, *Age of Discovery: Navigating the Storms of Our Second Renaissance*, revised paperback edition (London and New York: Bloomsbury Business, 2017), pp. 8, 46.

68   Satya Nadella, *Hit Refresh! The Quest to Rediscover Microsoft's Soul and Imagine a Better Future for Everyone* (William Collins, 2018, paperback), 106.

69   "What Policy Framework to Help Building Innovation and Growth into Europe's Capital Market?" a speech by Denis Beau at the AFME (Association for Financial Markets in Europe) Annual Capital Markets Technology and Innovation Conference in Paris, November 21, 2019: https://www.bis.org/review/r191122c.htm

70   "From AI to Facial Recognition: How China Is Setting the Rules in New Tech," *Financial Times*, October 7, 2020: https://www.ft.com/content/188d86df-6e82-47eb-a134-2e1e45c777b6

71   "China and US Compete to Dominate Big Data," *Financial Times,* May 1, 2018: https://www.ft.com/content/e33a6994-447e-11e8-93cf-67ac3a6482fd

72   "Why Millennials Are Driving Cashless Revolution in China," *Financial Times*, July 17, 2018: https://www.ft.com/content/539e39b8-851b-11e8-a29d-73e3d454535d

73   "Virtual Control: The Agenda Behind China's New Digital Currency," *Financial Times*, February 17, 2021: https://www.ft.com/content/7511809e-827e-4526-81ad-ae83f405f623

74   Nadella, *Hit Refresh!* p. 106.

75   United Nations Office on Drugs and Crime, "Money Laundering": https://www.unodc.org/unodc/en/money-laundering/overview.html

76   "Flipping the Odds of Digital Transformation Success," Boston Consulting

Endnotes

Group, October 29, 2020: https://www.bcg.com/en-gb/publications/2020/increasing-odds-of-success-in-digital-transformation

77　Milton Friedman first articulated his ideas on the purpose of business in his book, *Capitalism and Freedom* (University of Chicago Press, 1962), and reprised in a *New York Times* article in 1970 "A Friedman Doctrine—The Social Responsibility Of Business Is To Increase Profits," *New York Times*, September 13, 1970: https://www.nytimes.com/1970/09/13/archives/a-friedman-doctrine-the-social-responsibility-of-business-is-to.html

78　"Business Roundtable Redefines the Purpose of a Corporation to Promote 'An Economy That Serves All Americans'," Business Roundtable, August 12, 2019: https://www.businessroundtable.org/business-roundtable-redefines-the-purpose-of-a-corporation-to-promote-an-economy-that-serves-all-americans

79　Erin Meyer, *The Culture Map: Decoding How People Think, Lead, and Get Things Done across Cultures*, international edition (New York: Public Affairs, 2015)

80　For more on this, see "UK Targets Palestinian ICT & Telecoms," *InvestPalestine*, May 14, 2012: https://investpalestine.wordpress.com/2012/05/14/uk-targets-palestinian-ict-telecoms/

81　For more on the work of the Rewell Society, see: https://www.rewellsociety.org/

82　"Jeff Bezos: I've Made Billions of Dollars of Failures at Amazon," *Guardian*, December 3, 2014: https://www.theguardian.com/technology/2014/dec/03/jeff-bezos-billions-dollars-failures-amazon

83　Elon Musk News, "'If things are not failing, you are not innovating enough.' - Elon Musk," *Twitter*, October 9, 2017: https://twitter.com/elonmusknewsorg/status/917381643295428609?lang=en

84　Laurence G. Weinzimmer and Jim McConoughey, *The Wisdom of Failure: How to Learn the Tough Leadership Lessons without Paying the Price* (San Francisco: Jossey-Bass, 2013), p. 8.

85　Meyer, *The Culture Map*, p. 168.

86　Garry Kasparov, *How Life Imitates Chess: Insights into Life as a Game of Strategy* (London: Bloomsbury Publishing, 2007)

87　C. Raman, "The Colour of the Sea," *Nature*, 108, 367 (1921): https://www.nature.com/articles/108367a0

88　"Ask 'Why' Five Times About Every Matter," Toyota: www.toyota-europe.com/world-of-toyota/feel/quality

89　Antoine de Saint-Exupéry, *Le Petit Prince* (Paris, 1943)